FREE STATE BATTLEWAGON

U.S.S. Maryland (BB-46)

by Myron J. Smith, Jr.

Led by Maryland, the Pacific fleet, silhouetted against the western sun, steams out of New York harbor 13 March 1924 on its way to maneuvers off Panama. USN (NH 69200)

Pictorial Histories Publishing Company
Missoula, Montana

Library of Congress Catalog
Card No. 86-60435

ISBN 0-933126-76-X

First Printing April 1986
Second Printing April 1992
Third Printing November 1997

WARSHIP SERIES:
#1 U.S.S. West Virginia (BB-48)
#2 U.S.S. Pennsylvania (BB-38)
#3 U.S.S. California (BB-44)
#4 U.S.S. Maryland (BB-46)
#5 U.S.S. Tennessee (BB-43)

Front Cover: *Original painting of the U.S.S.* Maryland *by Paul Bender, Perth Amboy, N.J.*

Back Cover: *A postcard of the Armored Cruiser* Maryland.

PICTORIAL HISTORIES PUBLISHING COMPANY
713 SOUTH THIRD WEST
MISSOULA, MONTANA 59801

CONTENTS

Dedication: For Fred

INTRODUCTION

The battleship *Maryland* (BB-46) was the third, largest, and most famous ship to carry that name—and the last. She was christened in honor of the state of Maryland, whose star, the seventh, came into the Union on April 28, 1788, 70 days before the official ratification of the United States Constitution.

Affectionately dubbed "Old Mary" or "Fighting Mary," she also may have been called the "Old Line" or "Free State Battlewagon" in honor of that famous Continental infantry unit enshrined in the state's nickname. She was the pride of America and the world's most powerful dreadnought when commissioned in 1921, and the least damaged of all the battleships at Pearl Harbor on Dec. 7, 1941. Quickly into the thick of the Pacific war, the ship was under attack 100 times more—with the Japanese reporting her sunk on three different occasions. From beginning to end, the vessel remained a worthy symbol of the people and state whose spirit was put into words by James Ryder Randall and matched to the music of an old German hymn: "Maryland, My Maryland!"

FOREWORD

This foreword was originally penned by Captain J.D. Wilson for the *Maryland's* cruise-book, now long out-of-print. Because of its eloquence, we beg indulgence to employ it here as well.

This is a brief outline of the war history of a 24-year-old battleship, salvaged from the wreckage of Pearl Harbor. She was repaired and improved, to be damaged in action and repaired again and again, but each time coming back a better ship than before. Into her complex machinery and armament is woven the labor and skill of men and women from many walks of life, and at the end of hostilities more than 70 per cent of the men who manned her had been, at the beginning of the war, on farms, in schools, factories or professions. Yet, never was she so deadly an instrument of war as on the day peace was declared. Her record reflects the courage, determination, and resourcefulness of the American people.

J.D. Wilson
U.S.S. MARYLAND
November 1, 1945

The armored cruiser U.S.S. Maryland (CA-8) at sea, circa 1908.

FREE STATE BATTLEWAGON

THE FIRST MARYLAND, A SLOOP-OF-WAR

The first of three vessels to honor the state of Maryland had the shortest career and remains the most obscure, with neither plans nor illustrations of the vessel known to exist. In the 1790s, Congress reasoned that the merchants of America's great ports were the chief sufferers of the depredations of corsairs and privateers and ought to be willing, therefore, to make a special contribution to the defense of the U.S. merchant marine. Thus on June 30, 1798, the lawmakers authorized the Navy to accept any war-ships that the merchants might care to build and donate. The plan seemed agreeable to all parties and the new naval establishment received several excellent ships as a result.

Following a public subscription in the Baltimore area (mainly among the merchants), the hull for a three-masted warship of the sloop-of-war type was launched at the Prince Shipyard on June 3, 1799. According to correspondence from Henry Yellot, the Navy agent in Baltimore, the first *Maryland* was 87 feet long, had a moulded beam of 29 feet, and a 12- or 13-foot depth of hold. This "sharp-built" warrior was said to measure 380 tons. From a letter sent by James Buchanan and a letter to the Navy agent from the famous Capt. Thomas Truxton, we know that the *Maryland* had a spar deck and carried her many guns too low. The ship would, however, prove to be very fast in light weather and was generally regarded as a good sailer. Rated at 20 guns, the sloop may have carried anywhere from 26 to 36 cannons (ranging from 6- to 12-pounders), depending upon the records or accounts consulted.

"There was nothing exceptional about the *Maryland*," wrote her commander's biographer, "unless it was her carved work." Including a figurehead of the goddess of commerce and plenty, it was "quite elaborate, and . . . reflected no small honor on the progress of American arts." The sloop was accepted by the Navy in August 1799 and commissioned by Capt. (later commodore) John Rodgers, her first and only commander.

The *Maryland* served in the West Indies from October 1799 through late July 1800 as the U.S. fought an undeclared naval war with France. Patrolling the seas from French Guinea to Curacao in protection of American shipping, Rodgers' vessel did not take part in combat against Napoleon's privateers or men-of-war; however, she did win three prizes. The schooner *Clarissa*, an American slave-trader without papers, was taken on Jan. 4, 1800; and on July 26, the Portuguese brig *Gloria da Mar*, which had fallen to the French privateer *Cherry* 13 days earlier, was recaptured without a fight.

Departing Surinam in early August 1800, the *Maryland* returned to America via St. Kitts and St. Thomas. En route, she escorted a large convoy to safe waters and on Sept. 2 took the *Aerial*, a U.S. merchantman without papers. The *Maryland* was laid up in Baltimore over the winter for repairs, and Rodgers took his speedy command out of Chesapeake Bay in March 1801. Aboard was Congressman John Dawson, the U.S. envoy chosen to convey the revised and ratified Pickney Treaty to France. Arriving at Havre de Grace in April, the sloop was forced to remain in that port until July 15 when, because of difficulties in obtaining treaty ratification from Napoleon, Dawson sent her home. After delivering Dawson's dispatches and assistants, the *Maryland* was de-activated at Baltimore on Aug. 28 and her crew discharged. Just over a month later, on Oct. 2, 1801, Capt. Rodgers sold the first *Maryland* into private hands for $20,000.

THE ARMORED CRUISER
MARYLAND/FREDERICK (ACR/CA-8)

The next *Maryland* was the second of three armored cruisers authorized by the Naval Building Act of June 7, 1900. The ship was laid down by the Newport News Shipbuilding Co., of Newport News, Va., on Oct. 7, 1901, as Hull No. 39. Under the sponsorship of Miss Jennie Scott Watters, the ship was launched on Sept. 12, 1903. After the completion of her outfitting, the cruiser, sister to the *Colorado* (ACR-7) and *South Dakota* (ACR-9), was commissioned on April 18, 1905, with Capt. R.R. Ingersoll in command.

In a gleaming coat of white, the $3.8 million *Maryland* displaced 13,680 tons (normal load). She was 503 feet 11 inches long with a beam of 69 feet 7 inches and a mean draft of 24 feet 1 inch. Armor on the main belt ran 5-6 inches, depending on location, while steel protection on the turrets was 6 inches, with 9 inches on the conning tower. Her main armament consisted of four 8-inch guns in twin turrets, one fore and one aft of the superstructure. The secondary defenses featured 14 6-inch guns arranged in casemates (armored boxes), seven to a side, plus 18 3-inch "quick-firer" guns and two 18-inch submerged torpedo tubes. Two 3-inch anti-aircraft guns would be added in 1917.

The two-shaft, vertical 3-exp. reciprocating engines and BW, type WT, coal-fired boilers gave 23,000 indicated horsepower, sufficient for a seldom-achieved speed of 22 knots. Bunker space was provided for 2,075 tons of coal. The vessel was equipped with two military masts; the foremast would be removed in 1911 and replaced by a cagemast which, together with four tall funnels, proved to be the *Maryland's* most distinguishing features. Berths were provided for 47 officers and 728 enlisted men, although in the pre-World War I years recruiters would be lucky to send 370 volunteer bluejackets aboard plus a few Marines.

Following shakedown, Capt. Ingersoll's proud new charge joined the Atlantic Fleet for operations along the East Coast and in the Caribbean, including the winter 1905-06 fleet maneuvers near Cuba. In the spring of 1906, the cruiser paid a courtesy call on the port of Baltimore. There she received one of the best-known silver services ever to grace a U.S. warship. Consisting of 48 pieces, this $5,000 gift from the state of Maryland's citizens was exquisitely fashioned by master silversmiths, who carved into the plates and bowls hundreds of scenes depicting historic events and places around the state. In 1938, Capt. (later admiral) Harry W. Hill, who had been appointed the cruiser's gunnery officer in 1911, published a book detailing his 27-year study of the symbolism and significance of the various pieces. *Maryland's Colonial Charm, Portrayed in Silver* remains to this day the only hardback ever published exclusively about a warship's silver collection. After leaving Baltimore for a summer training cruise for naval militiamen, the *Maryland* put into Norfolk to join three sisters of Rear Adm. Willard H. Brownson's Armored Cruiser Squadron, which were preparing for a

Maryland being prepared for launching at the Newport News Shipbuilding and Drydock Company, Newport News, Virginia on 12 Sept. 1903. Note that portholes have not been drilled yet.
USN

September departure for the Asiatic Station.

Steaming through the Suez Canal with stops at Bombay, Colombo, and Singapore, the *Maryland* and her consorts came to anchor in the Yangtze River, below Shanghai, in late November 1906. Hardly had the anchors of his ships hit water when Adm. Brownson found himself facing a diplomatic crisis caused by an earlier misunderstanding over the treatment of certain Chinese businessmen in San Francisco. This confusion had led Tuan Fang, Empress Tzu Hsi's powerful and corrupt viceroy of Nanking, to foster a total boycott of all American imports throughout China's populous five southern provinces. Hoping to cause loss of face to the new American naval leader as he had to Brownson's predecessor, Tuan readily agreed to the admiral's request for a Nanking interview—something foreigners normally arrived at via land transport. Not to be outfoxed, Brownson elected to come by water and ordered his four large warships to move with much fanfare slowly up the Yangtze to Tuan's capital.

In full dress and accompanied by many of his similarly-attired officers, the squadron chief paid a formal call on the viceroy. During the courtesy-laden conference, Brownson almost offhandedly suggested that Tuan and his retinue might enjoy visiting aboard the cruisers. Fearful of what might happen if the invitation were refused, the Chinese leader, with 35 followers, fulfilled the American's suggestion a day later. The great cannon and smart gun drills visibly impressed Tuan, who went ashore knowing that he had been psychologically outmaneuvered. The boycott ended almost immediately. Brownson's gunboat diplomacy had succeeded without a shot being fired, but, just to make sure, his squadron remained near Chinese waters for most of the next year before returning to San Francisco.

The *Maryland* began a decade of routine Pacific service in the spring of 1908, participating in those training and flag-showing missions common to all units of the Armored Cruiser Squadron. Although the cruises were broken by various port visits and overhauls, life for most aboard in those "innocent years" often seemed one of hard work and never-ending drills: division maneuvering, target firing, director drills, mock attacks at night by torpedo boat flotillas, coaling (a filthy job), swabbing and polishing. Only sports and shore leave offered relief.

Among the highlights for the cruiser in this period was her transport of the secretary of state to Tokyo for the September 1912 funeral of Japan's Emperor Meiji Tenno and her two surveying missions to Alaska in 1912-13. On three occasions—in

Maryland with her new cage mast, 1910.

USN (NH 63761)

1913, 1914 and 1916—the *Maryland* steamed off the western Central American coast to aid, if necessary, Americans endangered by political turmoil in Nicaragua and Mexico.

On Nov. 9, 1916, the cruiser was renamed *Frederick* so that the "Maryland" name could be assigned to the newly-authorized battleship that would become BB-46. When war erupted with Germany on April 6, 1917, the *Frederick* was at sea en route to San Francisco from Puget Sound. Taking aboard a fresh draft of men and supplies, she departed the Golden Gate for the Atlantic.

The *Frederick's* first duty was patrol of the southeastern Atlantic, off the coast of South America. Here she guarded American and Allied shipping against possible attack by armed merchant cruisers or warships of the Central Powers. The *Frederick* was not tested in combat, but a review of the battles of Coronel and the Falkland Islands, fought in her sector by German and British armored- and battle-cruisers in October and December 1914, suggests the U.S. warship might have fared poorly had she met modern opponents. The *Frederick* was attached to Cruiser Division 2 at Norfolk in January 1918 and from February to November joined several of her sisters in the coastal escort of convoys east of the 37th meridian.

With the signing of the Armistice on Nov. 11, 1918, the tired old cruiser was converted into a troop transport. In six trans-Atlantic round trips between January and July 1919, she brought nearly 12,000 doughboys home from France. Reconverted to warship status at Philadelphia, the *Frederick* crossed the Atlantic once more in mid-1920 to drop off the U.S. Olympic team in Antwerp, Belgium, while conducting a naval reservist training cruise. Just after the fall elections, the cruiser steamed back to the Pacific, where she served as flagship, Train, Pacific Fleet, and conducted a lengthy cruise to South America in the spring of 1921. Operations off the U.S. West Coast occupied the remainder of her active duty career and on Feb. 14, 1922, she was decommissioned.

The second *Maryland*, which had represented America and the Free State at sea for almost 20 years, remained in the Mare Island reserve fleet until she was struck from the Naval Vessel Register on Nov. 13, 1929. A few months later, on Feb. 11, 1930, she was sold for scrap.

View taken while in drydock, 1911. Showing part of the crew repainting the ship's bottom.
USN (NH 50373)

"Amphitrite"   "His Majesty"   "Capt Ellicot"   "Baby"

©1912 R. McDaniel

"The Visit of the Royal Party" Maryland Crossing Equator 1912.

Top Left: Sailors using a sewing machine to improve the appearance of their hats, 1912. Note the parrot mascots.
USN (NH 50367)

Top Right: An early aerial kite target being readied for streaming, 1912.
USN (NH 50366)

Bottom: Visit of the "Royal Party" of "King Neptune" during the Crossing-The-Line ceremonies, 1912. Ship captain, Capt. Ellicot, appears in whites at the right of center.

USN (NH 50372)

At the end of World War One, the U.S.S. Frederick *(CA-8) (renamed in 1916) helped bring the troops home. Shown here docking in Hoboken, New Jersey, early 1919.*

USN (NH 50214)

U.S.S. MARYLAND (BB-46) CREATION

With a war raging in Europe and Japan restless in the Pacific, a great U.S. naval building program was authorized by Congress in 1916. American leaders planned to have the Navy, the nation's first line of defense, ready for whatever might happen. The Naval Act of Aug. 29, 1916, which was put on the books two months after the giant Anglo-German battleship encounter off Jutland, authorized 10 dreadnoughts and a host of lesser ships to be built within five years. Due to international complications, including the 1922 Washington Treaty, only three battleships would emerge from this legislation. Named either the *Colorado* class (for the earlier hull number) or the *Maryland* class (for the first ship laid down and commissioned), the three vessels were the final development in a series dating back to the 1913 *Pennsylvania* class.

The General Board was the U.S. Navy council that set the standards to which all American warships were designed between 1910 and 1945, and it laid great importance on the ability of battleships to operate together as a fleet, especially in the Pacific. This view was held by all Navy leaders from the chief of Naval Operations downward. As far as possible, these people insisted that successive designs be given similar speeds, radii of action, and handling/survivabilty qualities. This orderly process was not lost on U.S. lawmakers, who continually specified in their battlewagon authorization acts that new ships carry "as heavy armor and as powerful armaments as

any vessel of their class." Indeed, the General Board always advocated dreadnoughts that would equal or outclass the latest of Britain, Germany, or Japan. Pleased with their latest models, the *Tennessee* and *California*, the admirals naturally turned to blueprints of those vessels for inspiration.

When the "Fighting Mary" and her sisters, the *Colorado* (BB-45) and "Mountaineer Battlewagon" *West Virginia* (BB-48) were finished, they would be almost identical in appearance and propulsion to their immediate predecessors. The only real differences in the newer ships would be slightly thicker main belt armor and twin 16-inch turrets instead of the triple 14-inch mounts aboard the *Tennessee* class. In its authorization, Congress had specified that the ships of the *Colorado/Maryland* class, which were to be started "as soon as possible," were "not to exceed $11,500,000 each," less armor and armament. When the *Maryland* was commissioned in 1921, her total cost was $17,020,800.

Calling her "the most powerful battleship in the world," officials of the Bureau of Construction and Repair on Dec. 15, 1916, placed an order for the *Maryland's* construction with the Newport News Shipbuilding Co., the same firm that had completed the *Frederick* a decade earlier. The keel of the dreadnought, then known to the Navy as Battleship No. 46 and to the builders in Virginia as Hull 210, was laid down on April

Artist's conception by F. Miller, drawn about 1916, before the design was finally decided, of the battleships Colorado *(BB-45),* Maryland *(BB-46),* Washington *(BB-47) and* West Virginia *(BB-48).*

USN (NH 55271)

24, 1917, three weeks after the American declaration of war on Germany. The first frames were up within weeks and as inspectors checked the progress through 1917-20, thousands of workers, when not building more urgently needed escorts and merchantmen, took part in the project. Growing in size week by week, the vessel was skillfully hammered and riveted together. As the March 20, 1920, launch date approached, the craft, quite recognizable as a battleship, was over 60 percent complete.

Many prominent officials were on hand for the March 20 christening, a gala affair well covered by the state of Maryland's newspapers. Present were a variety of important fleet and civilian guests, including Navy Secretary Josephus Daniels and Maryland's chief executive, Albert C. Ritchie, as well as the state's two senators and six congressmen. In the ancient ceremony, sponsor Mrs. E. Brooke-Lee, wife of the state comptroller and daughter-in-law of Sen. Blair Lee, smashed the traditional champagne bottle across the ship's bow. This pre-arranged signal, greeted by loud cheering, sent the vessel, now officially U.S.S. *Maryland,* sliding down the greased ways. A month later, on April 12, the unfinished ship was reclassified as BB-46 under the Navy's new hull numbering system. Her outfitting continued for another year as the main belt armor was installed, the turrets built and guns put in place, and the superstructure and masts completed. Finally, early on the warm day of July 21, 1921, the sparkling new battleship, her brass polished and #5 gray paint still fresh in places, was ready to join the Navy.

Just after noon that sunny July day, the remainder of the ship's 62 officers, 70 Marines, and 1,022 enlisted men came aboard and, after stowing their gear, assembled at divisional parade on the quarterdeck aft. The American flag was hoisted on the flagstaff, the commissioning pennant was broken out at the main truck, and a band played the "Star Spangled Banner." The Norfolk yard commandant, after reading the formal commissioning directive, turned the ship over to Capt. Charles F. Preston. Reading his own orders aloud and after making a short address to the crew, the new skipper ordered the first watch set. Divisions were marched forward and within an hour, the *Maryland* was opened to a throng of visitors.

Maryland *under construction at Newport News, 1918.*   USN (NH 43100)

Ready for launching, 20 March 1920. Two tankers and another large ship are building on nearby slips.

USN (NH 93536)

Ready for launching at Newport News, March 1920.

USN (NH 69009)

PHYSICAL APPEARANCE

The most recent of Western battleships in 1921, the *Maryland*, as the first of her class commissioned, embodied the latest knowledge of naval architecture. Her armor, propulsion, compartmentation, and other features marked an advance over the designs of previous battlewagons, both U.S. and European. Labeled a "super-dreadnought" through much of her pre-Pearl Harbor career, the "Mary's" huge 16-inch guns (the first mounted in an American capital ship) made her at least equal in hitting power to the Japanese *Nagato*, which first took that caliber to sea in 1920.

A first line ship like the *Maryland*, sleek of hull with a clipper bow, had a long sweeping top deck covered with teak (which enlisted men were expected to holystone white) and a raised forecastle for the half length forward. Out of these rose the masts and funnels, the topside bridgework, and other structures collectively known as the superstructure. From the main deck, too, rose the bulky main turrets—great heavily armed forts holding the 16-inch guns. Each was mounted on top of roller-path bearings within a fixed armored tube called a barbette, a cylindrical structure extending vertically downward into the lower handling rooms and magazines. The ship's 5-inch/51 caliber secondary cannon jutted from casemates in the second of "02" deck.

Displacing 31,500 tons (normal load) or 33,590 tons (full load), the *Maryland* had an overall length of 624 feet (600 feet at the waterline), a beam of 94 feet, 3½ inches, and a mean draft of 29 feet, ⅔ inch, which could be extended to a maximum depth of hold of 35 feet. She was a bit longer than two football fields and as tall as an eight-story building.

The *Maryland*, like her two sisters and the *Tennessee*-class vessels, was known as an electric-drive ship. The main power plant consisted of eight electrically controlled, oil-burning Babcock and Wilcox boilers with a combined total heating surface of 41,768 square feet (plus 4,168 square feet superheated). The exhaust from this power plant rose through flue gas ducts to the two slim funnels directly overhead. The boilers were located in separate watertight compartments (four to port and four to starboard) under central control abeam the engine room. They produced steam under pressure of 250 pounds to the square inch, which expanded into a pair of large General Electric turbo-electric geared turbines, arranged in tandem on the centerline, along with six auxiliary turbo-generators.

Controlled by mechanical governors from one small compartment, the main generators sent 10,000 volts to the ship's four 62-ton, 12-foot diameter, 5,424 KW alternating-current motors, each of which was attached to a single propeller shaft. These motors were designed for 24 and 36 poles and featured wound rotors for both starting and running. At 170 rpm, each motor developed 7,000 horsepower. The estimated weight of all this machinery was 2,002 tons.

Although the *Maryland's* electric drive was identical to that aboard the *Tennessee* and *California*, its use via the six auxiliary turbines was much extended. Part of the steam generated by the boilers was diverted to those turbines which, in turn, supplied current to the anchor gear, refrigerating plant, and so forth. Her gun turrets were electrically maneuvered, the ammunition hoists were electric, and indeed every possible item of equipment—even the potato peelers—was run by electric power. The

Maryland delivered a total indicated shaft horsepower of 28,900 (compared with the 27,500 horsepower of the 1920 destroyer *Pruitt*), sufficient to provide power to a city of 100,000. It was reported by the press that during her high-speed "unofficial" trial runs over a mile course off Rockland, Maine, in 1921, she attained a top speed of 22.49 knots, "a new record for ships of her type."

The *Maryland's* normal fuel-oil capacity was 2,500 tons (over 700,000 gallons) with an unofficial maximum of 4,000 tons, enough to give an approximate range of 4,000 miles. Fuel consumption, at 17 knots, was 1.07 lb./shp, while the ship's tactical diameter (turning radius), with screws turning forward and full helm, was 700 feet. Course direction was controlled via a single rudder.

As with the machinery, the arrangement, thickness, and extent of armor and protective equipment on the *Maryland* corresponded to that on the ships of the *Tennessee* class. A waterline belt of 16-inch steel was designed to resist the penetration of a 16-inch shell fired from 16,000 yards. Extending 9 feet above the waterline and 8½ feet below, this belt was thickest abreast the turret magazines and amidships machinery. It tapered to 8 inches toward the ends and at its lower edge, closing with 14-inch transverse armored bulkheads.

Continuing the "all-or-nothing" protection concept begun with the *Nevada* (BB-36), designers agreed that due to stability requirements thick armor could not also be placed over the upper decks. Instead, they would minimize the effects of "plunging fire" by providing the ship with enough cover to absorb fragments from exploding shells. The deck armor extended over the machinery areas and steering gear. The outboard strakes of the upper deck were covered with 1½ inches of armor, the main deck amidships by 3½ inches, and the outboard strakes of the lower deck by 1½ inches, except for the region amidships, which received 2½ inches. To prevent flue gases from filling the ship in battle, the boiler uptakes were given 16 inches of steel covering at the funnel bases, tapering to 9 inches at the upper deck.

To aid in torpedo protection, the *Maryland* was given a 17-foot protective layer inboard of her belt. This layer was divided on each side of the hull by three unpierced bulkheads, each covered by ¼-inch steel plates. The large outer bulkhead was divided into five compartments inside the ship's skin; the three center compartments were filled with fuel oil while the two outer ones were left as air spaces.

Theoretically, the ship's skin would cause an incoming torpedo to explode. The compressed air in the first void would tend to absorb the expanding gases that were vented into the ship by the explosion and would distribute their force against bulkhead No. 1. The inertia of the oil in the three center compartments would, it was hoped, take up much of the shock, and the oil's incompressibility would cause bulkheads 2, 3, and 4 to help withstand the shock simultaneously with bulkhead 1. Compartment E was left as a compressible void so that bulkhead No. 5 would avoid the major shock, and instead serve as a flooding boundary in case bulkheads 2, 3, and 4 were ruptured. The oil in the center compartments, incidentally, was a part of the ship's fuel supply, but could be replaced by water as it was consumed.

Elsewhere, the main battery also was well guarded. The face of each 16-inch turret received 18 inches of steel while the sides and rear had 8 inches and the roof 5 inches. The barbette armor tapered in thickness as it descended behind the main belt, running 18 inches on the exposed sides, 16 inches on the tube, and 14 inches on the crown. Protection for the conning tower, from which the ship would be controlled in action, was 16 inches thick. The main armament directors also received 16 inches of protection, but it was much reduced for the high-angle directors.

The *Maryland's* main armament—her reason for being—consisted of eight 16-inch/45-caliber, 120-ton guns mounted in 1,245-ton superfiring twin turrets, two forward and two aft. Each of these 60-foot rifled giants had a maximum 30° elevation and could fire a 2,100-pound armor-piercing (AP) shell to a range of 34,500 yards, or about 19 miles, at an average, though well-practiced, rate of fire of 1.5 per minute.

The battleship's secondary armament, which was changed several times before Pearl Harbor and during World War II, initially consisted of fourteen 5-inch/51-caliber single-purpose "anti-destroyer" guns distributed seven to a side. Four were in open top deck mounts, two forward and two aft between the funnels, with 10 in second deck casemates. Additionally, four semi-automatic, 3-inch/50-caliber guns were carried for anti-aircraft protection, as well as a battery of saluting cannon, a field piece for the landing force, and various machine guns and small arms. The two 5-inchers located between the funnels were removed in 1922 and four more 3-inchers were added. All of the anti-aircraft guns were replaced in 1928-29 by eight 5-inch/25-caliber guns while in 1937-38, anti-aircraft protection was augmented by eleven 1.1-inch cannons. A pair of submerged 21-inch torpedo tubes that were aboard on commissioning day were found to be unworkable and were removed in 1928-29.

As built, the *Maryland* sported a pair of 140-foot lattice, or "cage," masts which supported large fire control tops, also known as "fighting" tops. With a large diameter at the base providing support, each mast was formed from two inclined sets of steel tubing (clamped together at intersections) which make up rigid sets of triangles. The enclosed mast tops housed the main and secondary control stations, the latter one level below the former. Complementing the main battery director atop the bridge was a second one on No. 2 16-inch turret. It was once atop No. 3 but removed to allow aviation experiments aft. For a few years, a director also was carried on a mainmast platform.

The secondary directors had platform locations, one on either side of the lower level of the tops. In support of communications gear, each mast also sported large yardarms and hinged topmasts with small yardarms. A platform encircling the main mast carried four large search lights, and after 1937-38, each mast top had two small platforms (one facing forward and one aft) equipped with single anti-aircraft machine guns.

These two masts were the ship's most distinguishing pre-war characteristics. They were also fitted aboard her sisters and the *Tennessee*-class ships and distinguished "Mary" from the rest of the battleship force as a member of the so-called "Big Five."

The *Maryland* was the first U.S. battlewagon to be permanently fitted with an aircraft catapult. Shortly after the ship's acceptance, the Bureau of Aeronautics requested that a compressed air turntable model be mounted on her fantail, where it could be serviced by a simple derrick (later replaced by a crane). From this step, which in 1922 resulted in the first successful catapulting of a service-type aircraft, the editorial staff of the ship's newspaper was provided with a readymade title for its publication, "The Catapult." During the 1928-29 refit, a second catapult was fitted atop No. 3 turret where it could be serviced by the cranes that handled cargo and the small craft stacked amidships.

Each pre-war Battleship Division had an assigned observation (VO) squadron of the same number, with a three-plane section on each ship. In late 1940, for example, the *Maryland* was the third ship of BatDiv 4, so her air unit was the third section of VO-4. The three aircraft on board would vary in type over the years, but were always stowed atop the catapults, there being no enclosed hangars. By October 1940, the *Maryland* was equipped with Vought OS2U-1 Kingfishers, the tails of which were painted black, VO-4's distinguishing color.

With the limited peacetime funding that followed the Washington Treaty, which limited construction, the U.S. Navy began the reconstruction of its active battleships, the older ones first. Funds for the modernization of the *Maryland* and her sisters was authorized in April 1939, but in view of the situation in Europe and the Far East, it was decided to hold off on rebuilding them. Thus held in a state of readiness, only minor improvements, not taking much time, were allowed. In 1940-41, "Mary" received a pair of large anti-aircraft control instruments, located one on either side of the forward cage mast, to replace her small rangefinders. The 5-inch/25s on each side of the shelterdeck forward were removed while the remainder were fitted with auxiliary protective shields as well as splinter screens that extended to the height of the railings.

Vought VE-7 Seaplane catapulted from Maryland, *1925.*   USN (NH 44636)

Top Left: In drydock at Hunters Point, California, 13 Nov. 1928, being readied for President-Elect Herbert Hoover's goodwill tour of South America.

USN (NH 69091)

Top Right: Arrival of Hoover aboard Maryland *at San Pedro, California, 19 Nov. 1928 to 5 Jan. 1929.*

USN (NH 00840)

Bottom: Crossing the equator during Hoover's trip.
USN (NH 000724)

OPERATIONAL HISTORY THROUGH P.H. 1921-1941

After her July 21, 1921, commissioning, America's "Queen of the Seas" paid a courtesy call on the citizens of her name state. Arriving in Baltimore in early August, Capt. Preston and his men proudly exhibited the new battleship to thousands of impressed Marylanders and, in a brief ceremony, accepted the famous silver set that had graced the wardroom of the old armored cruiser. The drills and trials of the East Coast shakedown cruise that followed must surely have contrasted with this first of many port visits. After trials, the *Maryland* put in at Norfolk where she became the flagship of Adm. Hilary P. Jones. During the next several months, her fate and that of capital ship aviation became closely tied.

During the spring of 1922, the *Maryland's* aircraft catapult was perfected and tested. In late May, a new VE-7SF observation plane, first design of the Lewis and Vought Corp. (later Chance-Vought), was brought on board and Preston's command moved to a trial position off Yorktown, Va. There, on May 24, routine operation of catapults aboard U.S. warships is said to have begun. The Vought, piloted by Lt. Andrew C. McFall with Lt. (later admiral) Dewitt C. Ramsey as passenger, was successfully launched and recovered.

This battlewagon shot would lead the Navy to install catapults on other dread-noughts and to operate aircraft from existing capital ships. The flight demonstrated the capabilities of warplanes to officers and men throughout a fleet that was less than air-minded. Techniques developed aboard the *Maryland* and her sisters would allow the expansion of air support for surface and amphibious forces. These techniques included methods for gunfire spotting and experiments with aerial tactics that later were more fully developed by carrier aviation. A VE-7SF also made the Navy's first carrier takeoff from the flight deck of the *Langley* (CV-1) on Oct. 17, 1922, about five months after the "Mary's" success.

With the commissioning of the sister ships *Colorado* (BB-45) and *West Virginia* (BB-48) still more than a year away, the *Maryland*, due to her size and newness, was much in demand for special occasions in the months following the McFall/Ramsey flight. She appeared at Annapolis in early June to participate in the festivities surrounding the 1922 Naval Academy graduation. Between June 17 and July 10, the ship was in Boston for the anniversary of Bunker Hill and for the Fourth of July celebration. Open house gave many residents of Massachusetts the opportunity to come aboard. Adm. Jones, Capt. Preston, officers and men reeled off to distinguished guests and ordinary citizens the ship's statistics. The great guns and the huge 10-ton

Profile, 1920s.   USN (NH 46417)

Off of Yorktown, Virginia, 1923.   NA (80-CF-2057-12)

anchors, to say nothing of the towering cage masts, were gasped at by thousands.

The first of many diplomatic missions for the *Maryland* came that fall when, between Aug. 18 and Sept. 25, she transported Secretary of State Charles Evans Hughes to Brazil as the U.S. representative to that nation's brilliantly-celebrated Centennial Exposition. In Rio harbor, Preston's ship played host to officers from the visiting warships of over a dozen nations, including Great Britain and Japan.

In the spring following her return from Brazil, the *Maryland* steamed to Panama to pick up the visiting navy secretary, Edwin Denby, and make her first appearance with other units of the battleship fleet. Sailing into Panama Bay with Denby, Jones, and other dignitaries on board, the "Mary" participated in a series of March 23 naval maneuvers designed to show off the proficiency of America's dreadnoughts. The exercise culminated with the sinking by gunfire of the Navy's first radio-controlled target ship, *Coast Battleship No. 4,* formerly the *Iowa* (BB-4). As the sea rushed into the gaping holes along the waterline and the target ship turned turtle to starboard, Secretary Denby ordered the *Maryland's* band to strike up the national anthem, the last strains of which "floated over the placid bay just as the tip of the *Iowa's* nose settled beneath

the waves." After delivering Denby and Jones to America, where the latter transferred his flag to the *Pennsylvania* (BB-38), the *Maryland* steamed through the Panama Canal in late June to join the Battle Fleet stationed on the West Coast.

Peacetime service for the Battle Fleet (renamed the Battle Force in 1931), United States Fleet, involved an annual cycle of maintenance, training, and readiness exercises. Each year the dreadnought divisions of this group took part in competitions in engineering performance and gunnery, as well as an annual fleet problem (war game). Beginning with her 1923 appearance in Fleet Problem I and continuing with few interruptions through Fleet Problem XXI in April 1940, the *Maryland* held a prominent position in these battle exercises.

Her proficiency often came though in the keen competition between individual battleships. She won the Fleet Engineering Trophy in 1924 and again in 1932. In November 1926, the *Maryland* conducted experimental firing with the Ford Instrument Co.'s new Mk. XIX anti-aircraft fire control system, which incorporated a stabilized line of sight to aid in the tracking of approaching aircraft. During the competitive year of 1927-28, the *Maryland* won the Gunnery "E" for excellence. The prized Battle Effic-

Top Left: In the Gaillard Cut, Panama Canal, 13 Feb. 1923.
USN (NH 73833)

Top Right: In the Miraflores Locks, Panama Canal, 1934.
NA (80-CF-2057-7)

Bottom: In San Francisco Bay, 1930.   NA (80-CF-2057-1)

iency Pennant, the "Meatball," was hoisted in 1930 when the ship had the highest combined score in the gunnery and engineering competition, although the *New Mexico* (BB-40), having tied the score, also received a "Meatball" streamer.

It was in athletics, an area important to morale, that the *Maryland* had few peers. From the beginning her sportsmen made strong bids for supremacy in each of the Navy's sports competitions. The football team was Battleship Division Champion in 1928 and 1930 and took the Battle Force Championship in 1932. In 1930, the "Mary" captured the Fleet Basketball Championship while the following year, her raceboat crew took the annual cup race on Lake Washington. In 1933, the greatest athletic glory of all, the General Excellence Athletic Trophy, nicknamed the "Iron Man," came aboard and was much prized by officers and bluejackets alike.

From July to September 1925, the *Maryland* participated in the successful Battle Fleet tour to Australia and New Zealand. At liberty in those nations' ports, her crewmen not only drank in a Prohibition-free atmosphere, but also played soccer and baseball with their ANZAC hosts.

The *Maryland's* most important diplomatic mission took place in the late fall of 1928. Shortly after his election, Herbert Hoover asked President Calvin Coolidge for the loan of a battleship to make a goodwill tour of South America. After years of imperialism and "Dollar Diplomacy," Hoover recognized that the "United States, to put it mildly, was not popular in the rest of the Hemisphere." Coolidge suggested in

turn that the former commerce secretary take a cruiser because "it would not cost so much," but wanting room for his retinue, Hoover held out until the chief executive agreed to allow him transport south in the *Maryland*.

San Pedro harbor was adorned with bunting and brass as the president-elect, his wife and followers, boarded the *Maryland* on Nov. 20. As the ship gathered way to the sound of saluting guns, the Hoovers retired to their cabin in the fantail stern. There they were doubtless pleased to see that the famous silver service had been broken out and placed in a special glass case for their examination while the cabin also held the first vanity dresser ever installed on a U.S. warship.

Following a map drawn by the late Adm. George Dewey, the *Maryland* dropped anchor off Cape San Lucas, Baja, Calif., to give Mr. Hoover, a noted angler, the opportunity to try out his luck and his new fishing gear. Two launches were lowered for a late afternoon expedition with a third, personally led by the battleship's skipper, Capt. Victor A. Kimberly, along as guardboat. Trolling first with a spinner and then with a silver minnow, Hoover hopefully—and vainly—watched the launch's wake awaiting the strike of an amberjack or marlin, but the game fish were not hitting. Finally, a dolphin struck the president-elect's line, and a second grabbed the line of fishing companion and columnist Mark Sullivan. With utter disregard for White House etiquette, the Sullivan fish ran across the Hoover line and fouled it, causing Hoover to lose the new reel from his new rod. Allan Hoover, fishing in the second boat, was no

Broadside view, 23 Aug. 1935.   USN

more successful than his father, and his mother lost a bet on the angling proficiency of her men.

As the *Maryland* steamed between ports, Mr. Hoover, wearing a Navy chief yeoman's cap, filled his days with constitutionals around the deck, reclining on a lounge to chat with the 20 newspapermen aboard, reading detective stories, dictating memos, and observing the workings of the battleship, especially its range finders and fire control instruments. As the *Maryland's* signalmen radioed hundreds of stories and press releases home, the ship's officers, as hosts, took up shuffleboard, deck golf, and trapshooting. Evenings were spent on the quarterdeck viewing some of the 50 new films Cecil B. DeMille had personally given the Hoovers in San Pedro, with all off-duty men invited to the screenings.

During the Nov. 30 showing, as the *Maryland* moved through the Gulf of Tehuantepec, a great storm arose sending everyone to shelter. One wave smashed a port in the Hoovers' quarters, flooding their dining room but sparing the silver set. The heavy seas kept the president-elect up all night, and, dressed in a bathrobe, he used the time to explore the ship. Soon after sunrise, the Hoovers joined Capt. Kimberly on the bridge to admire the ship's handling in the still-towering seas.

Following stops at Honduras, El Salvador, and Nicaragua, the *Maryland* crossed the Equator. To mark the occasion, a piratical visitor calling himself Davy Jones, representative of King Neptune, clambered over the side. He bore warrants for the arrest of 800 of the 1,300 crewmen and guests aboard. The president-elect and his wife were exempt as Hoover was already a 14-crossing "shellback" with more voyages to his credit than any other man aboard save his naval aide, Cmdr. A.T. Beauregard.

All night the ship echoed with commotion as "pollywogs" (guests, officers, and enlisted men alike) were captured and sent to the brig. At 9 a.m. the following day, the parade of prisoners began and the neophytes were hauled before the Royal Court to hear the verdicts of King Neptune's judges—the Hoovers. The first to face charges was Allan Hoover, who was quickly found guilty. A royal bootlegger then administered a soup of vinegar and pepper from a whiskey bottle and the youth was then lathered with lampblack, shaved with a wooden razor, dumped into a water tank, and beaten as he moved down a gauntlet of cotton clubs. Similar treatment awaited the others—and thousands more as this ceremony was repeated during every Equator crossing of the ship's lifetime.

The *Maryland's* voyage continued with additional stops at Ecuador, Peru, Chile, Argentina, and Uruguay. At Montevideo, the Hoovers transferred to the *Utah*(BB-31) for continuation to Brazil and then to home. Commentators at the time hailed the *Maryland's* mission, and Hoover is generally acknowledged as the originator of a policy which his successor, Franklin Roosevelt, would call the "Good Neighbor" policy. As chief executive, Hoover saw the *Maryland* only once more, during the fleet review put on for his benefit off the Virginia Capes in May 1930.

Throughout the 1930s, in the Pacific and occasionally the Atlantic, the *Maryland* continued her training and readiness duties. Exercises were met and dignitaries received on board. As in 1927 and 1930, she participated in presidential fleet reviews, including those of 1934 and 1939. Cities along the American coasts that were celebrating centennials or other festivals often found the huge warship holding open house in their ports.

Passing through the entrance to the Pearl Harbor Naval Base, Hawaii, 1937.

NA (80-CF-7973-12)

During the spring of 1940, Fleet Problem XXI was conducted in Hawaiian waters. At the conclusion of the exercise, the Battle Force did not, as was its practice, return to San Pedro. In hopes that a strong signal might deter the Japanese from Far Eastern expansion, President Roosevelt, over the objections of CINCUS Adm. James O. Richardson (shortly thereafter relieved by Adm. Husband E. Kimmel) ordered his battleships to remain based at Pearl Harbor.

During the spring and summer of 1940, the U.S. command sought capability for fleet replenishment at sea and to this end began a series of tests for its different ship classes. After the execution of Roosevelt's order to hold the Battle Force at Hawaii, the *Maryland* was designated to undergo refueling exercises as representative of all the battleships. Once workers at the Pearl Harbor Navy Yard had made alterations for fittings and equipment, the ship took part in a successful underway refueling from the tanker *Brazos* (AO-4) on July 31. Although no difficulties were encountered in the oil transfer, the *Brazos'* rudder suddenly jammed as she was conducting post-refueling zig-zag maneuvers alongside the *Maryland* and she was slightly damaged forward in the resulting collision with the battleship.

From late 1940 to Dec. 7, 1941, the *Maryland*, with time out for an overhaul trip to the West Coast, carried out a schedule of training with other BatDiv 4 units of Vice Adm. William S. Pye's Battle Force (Task Force 1). Basing on Pearl Harbor, Pye's group participated in a number of two-week evolutions at sea in the Hawaiian operating area, each followed by a week in port for upkeep. Commanded by Capt. E.W. McKee for most of those months, the *Maryland* received a new skipper, Capt. D.C. Godwin, on Nov. 21, 1941. Godwin assumed command just in time to participate

View of America's Pacific naval power in the late 1930s. Maryland *leads the procession. Japanese authorities were alarmed by this growing sea threat.*

USN (NH 50260)

in Pye's last exercise before the Pearl Harbor attack.

The final pre-war cruise of the Battle Force was executed under combat conditions. Battle stations aboard the *Maryland* and her consorts were maintained under conditional watches as the ships practiced evasive actions against simulated enemy attack. Ships operated darkened and destroyers were ordered to attack any submarines outside of the sanctuary areas of the U.S. boats. Although the ships practiced circular task group formations, the majority of the dreadnoughts' exercises were in type maneuvers, especially of the Turn 9 or 9 Corpen variety. The ability of a battleship to turn exactly in the wake of the ship ahead was deemed to be of critical importance, as was keeping a proper distance at night. Gun and fire drills were held, but careful attention to exercises in anti-aircraft gunnery, damage control, and shore bombardment were generally lacking. On Dec. 5 at the conclusion of the fortnight evolution, the long, gray line of battlewagons put into Pearl Harbor, maneuvering up around Ford Island and down to the southeast side of a series of masonry mooring quays ("keys") often known as "Battleship Row." The strict regulation observed at sea was relaxed as the crews of the battleships engaged in their regular in-port routines.

Japanese secret agent Takeo Yoshikawa reported late on Dec. 6 that the units of the Battle Force were quiet. Torpedo nets, he noted, were not drawn around any of the ships (none were available) and aerial surveillance had been nil. Sunday dawn found the *Maryland* moored, as she had been all weekend, at Quay 5 with some 40 to 60 feet of water under her keel. Alongside to port was the *Oklahoma* (BB-37), with lines and gangway connecting the two. Ahead was moored the *California* (BB-44), while astern the *Tennessee* (BB-43) and the *West Virginia* (BB-48) were similarly tied together. The bows of the battleships all pointed toward the harbor entrance, with the *Maryland* and *Oklahoma* positioned at the head of the channel that extended past the officers' club to the submarine base.

It was a fairly quiet morning and the *Maryland*, like her sisters, lay in Readiness Condition Three (or "X")—two machine guns manned and two 5-inch/25s prepared with ready ammunition and crews. Those officers and men not sleeping, reading, or playing cards were finishing breakfast or getting ready for liberty at 0900 ashore in Honolulu. Other men already were ashore, preparing to return aboard from leave granted the previous evening.

Japanese photograph of the attack on Pearl Harbor 7 Dec. 1941. The Maryland *is inboard of the overturned* Oklahoma. USN

U.S.S. Maryland
Orders for the Day

Sunday, December 7, 1941 — Pearl Harbor, T.H.

	Until 1200	After 1200
Head of Department:	Lt. Cdr. HADLEY	Lt. Cdr. CRONIN
	Until 1100	After 1100
Staff Duty Officer:	Cdr. FITZGERALD	Cdr. HAMILTON

Duty Section Officers: 4th.
Duty and Standby Section Crew: 4th. and 2nd.
Duty Division: 4th.
Military and Medical Guardship: MARYLAND
Relief Military and Medical Guardship: NEVADA
Guard Mail Petty Officer: Watson D.A. Cox
Duty Boats: 2nd. Motor Boat.
4th. and 2nd. Motor Launches
No. 2 Motor Whaleboat.

0000 Daily routine with the following changes:

0600 Reveille.
Send 6 hands from anchor watch in stores boat equipped with cargo net to pick up ice at stores landing.

0630 Scrub down weather decks.

0730 Breakfast for crew.
Call from duty division 4 hand cleaning detail equipped with buckets, scrubbers and brooms to report to Fleet Landing at 0800.

0800 Turn to—Duty Division rig church in 1st. Division part of ship.

0830 Send Catholic Church Party to U.S.S. OKLAHOMA.

0900 Hoist guard flags (military and medical).

0910 Liberty commences.

0930 Quarters for muster.

0950 Send Motor Launch with crew and equipment to act as patrol boat to report to Commander Base Force by 1000.

0955 Sound Church Call.

0959 Toll ships bell one minute.

1000 Protestant divine services in 1st. div. part of ship.

1100 Send temporary patrol ashore (2P01c and 2P02c)

1930 Movies.

J.M. HAIMES, Commander, U.S. Navy, Executive Officer.

Just before 0800, 182 warplanes commenced their well-planned attack from the six carriers of Vice Adm. Chuichi Nagumo's First Naval Air Fleet. As bombs rained down on the Ford Island air station, Rear Adm. P.N.L. Bellinger, naval air chief, broadcast one of the most electrifying messages of American history: "Air Raid Pearl Harbor—This is No Drill!"

The excitement and noise from the island brought the *Maryland's* crew topside. Just as the attack started, Seaman 1/c Leslie V. Short, in one of the foremost machine gun stations, broke off addressing Christmas cards and witnessed smoke and flames rising from an air base building. Breaking out nearby ammunition, he quickly loaded his .50-caliber Browning and opened fire on two strangely-marked torpedo bombers that were launching against the *Oklahoma*, downing one. As more aircraft bore in from the southeast, the *Marylanders* realized that this was not a U.S. exercise. Jarring explosions came from the thrice-torpedoed *Oklahoma*, while the *Maryland's* boatswain mate of the watch piped "Away Fire and Rescue Party," the bugler blew General Quarters, and the emergency klaxon rang steadily.

Word of the Japanese attack passed excitedly through the ship; one man burst into the CPO wardroom to announce: "The Japs are here!" A few of the anti-aircraft batteries initially had joined Short, but as more bombers appeared, most of the *Maryland's* anti-air defense sped into operation. Ammunition lines were manned and wondering chaos gave way to determined opposition. Dozens of men climbed aboard from the stricken *Oklahoma*; many were covered in oil, but most rushed to help fire the guns. About this time, the *Arizona* (BB-39) blew up in a huge spout of flame. A number of escaping sailors fell into the water as the rapidly rising lines from BB-37 began to pop.

Not long after the "Abandon Ship" order was given and within 20 minutes of the raid's beginning, the *Oklahoma*, having taken two more torpedoes, capsized to 150 degrees. The gallant old ship's masts went into the mud and the starboard side of her bottom appeared above water, the keel and propeller shaft in clear view. Electricians Mate Harold North on the *Maryland* uttered a silent prayer; Friday night he and his mates had cursed as the *Oklahoma* tied up alongside, shutting off the night breeze. The ships astern the *Maryland* were obscured by thick, black smoke and raging flames, but it appeared that the *West Virginia* was sinking. Oil on the surface astern burned fiercely and several times threatened to drift down on Godwin's ship.

During a lull in the attack, Rear Adm. Walter S. Anderson and members of his Bat-Div 4 staff returned. Anderson and his men would take charge of immediate salvage opportunities and relay messages from Adm. Kimmel to other ships around the anchorage. Anderson hardly was aboard when additional Japanese aircraft approached "Battleship Row," intent upon killing those inboard ships which torpedoes had been unable to reach. Fifty bombers came in to drop 16-inch AP shells (from the *Nagato*) which had been converted into aerial bombs through the addition of tail fins. The Japanese planes flew from the port side through dense smoke to drop their loads, but their aim was rendered inaccurate by an increasing blizzard of American anti-aircraft shells.

The *Maryland* was hit by two of the Japanese bombs, both of which had a low level of detonation that resulted in relatively little damage. The first plowed through the forward awning and splintered on the forecastle. The bomb opened a hole about 2 feet by

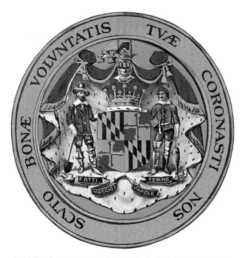

THE GREAT SEAL OF MARYLAND

USS MARYLAND — 1935
Drawn by Alan B. Chesley, 1986
Scale = 1:500

OUTBOARD PROFILE

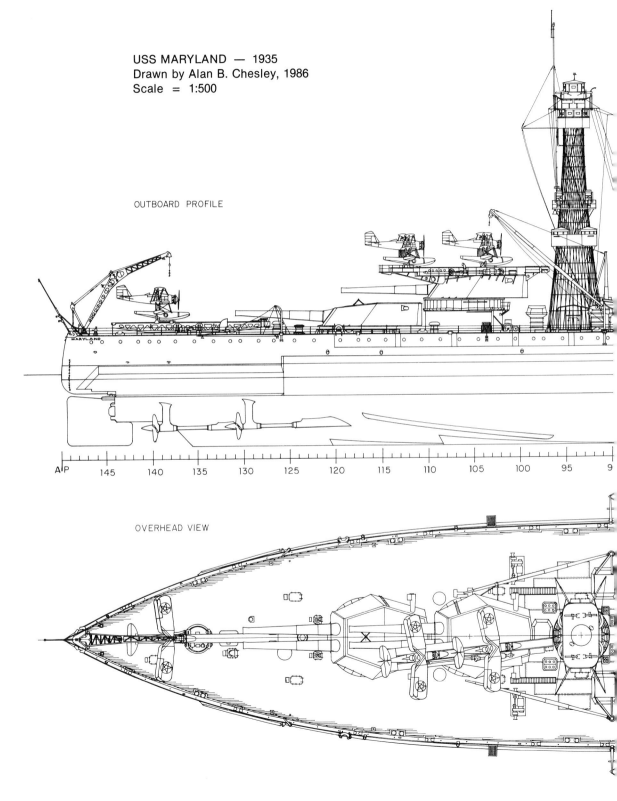

OVERHEAD VIEW

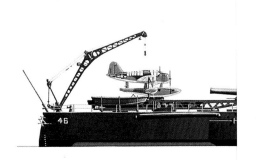

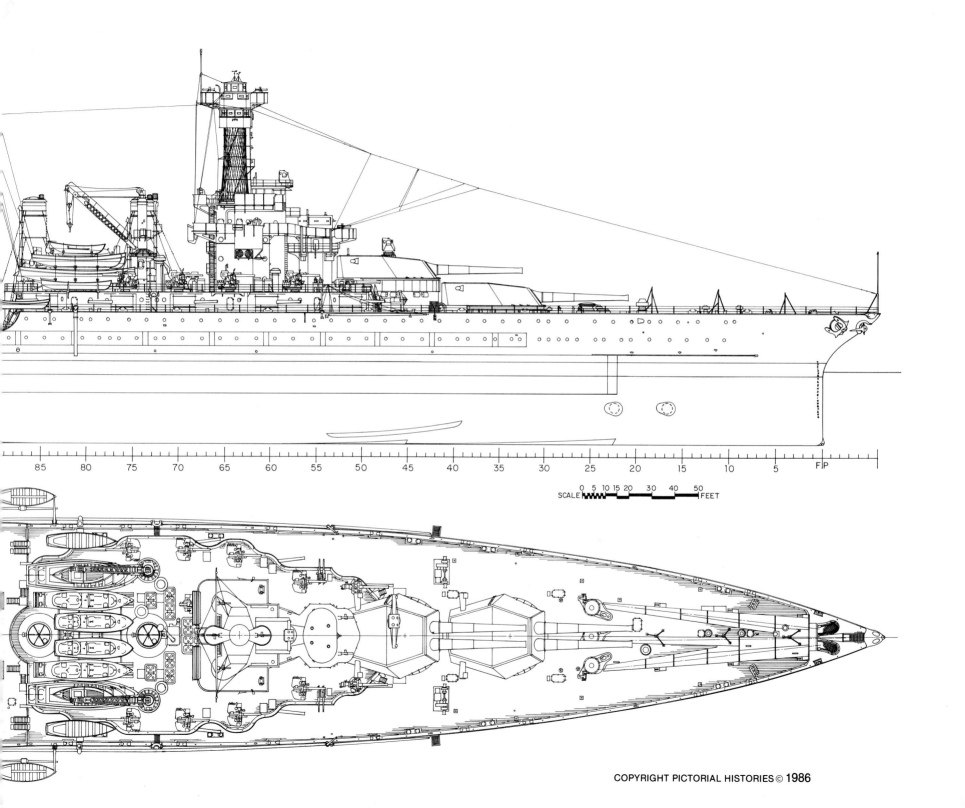

85   80   75   70   65   60   55   50   45   40   35   30   25   20   15   10   5   F P

SCALE |||||| 0 5 10 15 20   30   40   50 | FEET

20 feet and caused damage in compartments below. The awning fire was soon extinguished, although on at least one occasion, the damage control party was forced to seek shelter from strafing Zeros. The second bomb slanted into the hull at the 22-foot level at frame 10 and exploded in the hold, causing significant flooding which lowered the bow some 5 feet. Still, "Mary" was very lucky. She suffered less physical damage during the raid than any of the other battleships, and her casualties—two officers and two enlisted men dead—were the lightest. The damages and deaths she suffered later in the war would make Pearl Harbor appear almost a picnic. Despite this ship's splendid survival, enthusiastic Japanese propagandists boasted later in the day that she had been irretrievably sunk.

Throughout the Japanese second wave attack, the *Maryland's* gunners kept up their spirited defense. Four enemy aircraft were claimed destroyed in addition to Seaman Short's, including three downings shared with the cruiser *Helena* (CL-50). When the raid was over, a check showed an expenditure of 7,450 rounds of anti-aircraft ammunition.

As the port remained alert for a possible third wave, many of the *Maryland's* sailors joined firefighting parties to help quell the blazes on the more critically hurt ships nearby. Others assisted in the desperate efforts to save men trapped in the overturned *Oklahoma*. Tapping from within helped shipfitters locate a dozen places to cut holes in the sunken ship's hull. Many sailors were released and then taken directly to the *Maryland's* sick bay. One survivor came up in total shock, clutching a basketball which he refused to surrender even to the doctors. As a result of these and other efforts, 32 crewmen were extracted from the *Oklahoma*. Meanwhile, rumors about the battle spread everywhere; at one point, the *Maryland's* public address system wrongly announced that two Japanese carriers were sunk. Throughout the late morning and into the afternoon, the *Maryland's* band, assembled on the quarterdeck, played vigorously in an effort to keep spirits up.

When equipment became available, the *Maryland's* flooding storerooms were pumped out and patches placed. On Dec. 11, she was removed from behind the *Oklahoma's* hulk and moved to the navy yard for repairs. Readied for action without need of dry-docking, she departed for Bremerton on Dec. 20 accompanied by the *Pennsylvania* (BB-38) and *Tennessee* (BB-43). Emerging from the Puget Sound yards in February 1942, the *Maryland* became the first of the damaged Pearl Harbor battleships to return to active service.

The Pearl Harbor attack led to changes in the *Maryland's* appearance. On Dec. 30, 1941, she arrived for emergency upgrading at the Puget Sound Navy Yard, Bremerton, Wash. In order to have an additional battleship available as soon as possible, basic overhaul work and some vital modifications were rapidly completed.

Steel-helmeted yard workers immediately began construction of shallow (about 6½ feet) bulges on both sides of the ship, gradually tapering them toward bow and stern. These "blisters" formed a kind of second hull that covered the side armor from below the waterline to the upper deck and provided increased stability and better torpedo protection. As a result, the battleship's beam was widened to 108 feet, a girth which would now allow her to pass through the locks of the Panama Canal with just inches to spare.

The after cage mast was cut off at the height of the funnels and 20mm Oerlikon anti-aircraft cannon were mounted on a platform fitted atop the stump. A short topmast with an inclined flagstaff was braced to the forward edge of this top platform while an additional platform rim was located below the searchlight position. The aircraft catapult was removed from No. 3 turret to make room for two platforms, each equipped with two 20mms. The pre-war catapult gear on the fantail was refurbished, as was its crane. The ship received four new Kingfisher observation planes, sometimes called the "Quarterdeck Messerschmitts." The 5-inch/25s were all replaced by eight modern 5-inch/38-caliber "dual purpose" pieces. As no turrets were yet available, these were fitted with the protective shields and screens that had guarded the old cannon. Although the casemated 5-inch/51s remained, the two mounted on the deck below the bridge were removed to provide space for "tub" mounts, each containing a quadruple 40mm Bofors. Additional 40mms were placed in other key positions, bringing the total at this refitting to 16.

Rapid-fire 20mms, which critics would later call ineffective against Japanese warplanes but great for crew morale, were spotted all over the main deck: two forward of No. 1 turret, two on each side of No. 2 turret, three on each side of No. 3 turret, and 14 (in two positions of 4 and 3) overhanging the main deck rail port and starboard. Added to these were a dozen more 20mms atop two "flying platforms" constructed on either side of the forward funnel, which now received a slanted cap. Radar equipment ("SC" for air search and Mk. 3 main battery control) was installed in the foretop, above which were the appropriate antennas, while the main battery rangefinder atop No. 2 turret was removed.

When the ship departed the yard on Feb. 26, 1942, her hull was painted in low-visibility "sea blue" (in accordance with camouflage scheme Measure 11), a color that blended well with the ocean and afforded more protection at night.

The *Maryland* received a second reconstruction at Bremerton in the spring of 1944. This time the stump of the after cage mast was replaced by a prefabricated, multi-level tower superstructure fitted with two Mk. 3 main battery directors, the foretop losing its 16-inch instrument. A simple, reinforced, yardarm-crossed pole mast was fitted to this after tower and equipped with a type "SG" surface search radar antenna. The forward cage mast was retained, but could hardly be recognized as such due to a high bridge structure and the huge foretop. The radar equipment on the forward mast was extended and included one antenna each for types "SK" and "SRa." Two "FD" secondary battery directors were installed on a bridgetop platform, one flanking each side of the foremast, while deck protection throughout was improved and the ship's suit of 40mms was increased to a total of 48. The combined weight of all modifications raised the *Maryland's* displacement to 34,000 tons (39,000 full load).

When she sailed from Bremerton this second time, her hull was painted in the dazzle-pattern of Measure 32. Pale-gray, haze-gray, and navy-blue mat covered all horizontal surfaces in a widely-employed scheme designed to provide additional protection against aerial attack. The battlewagon's identification numbers were painted on the hull fore and aft, but were purposely made very small.

The victim of extensive kamikaze attacks late in the conflict, the *Maryland* returned to the Washington yards once again on May 7, 1945. For the next three and one-half months, she was overhauled and her battle damages repaired. During this final rebuilding, the ship was extensively remodeled topside. All of the free-standing and casemated 5-inchers were replaced by 16 5-inch/38s in eight double turrets, four to a side on the main deck. The 20mm armament, which by now had grown to a total of 37 pieces, was reduced to 18 through the removal of the "flying platforms" and other positions. The latest air search radar equipment was installed along with Mk. 8 main battery instruments. Internal construction resulted in bunks for the crew instead of the cots or hammocks formerly used. The *Maryland* emerged in August as powerful as she ever was going to be, but during shakedown tests, the war ended.

Views taken during the Pearl Harbor attack with the Oklahoma *overturned and the* Tennessee *in the background.*

USN (NH 83065) Left; USN (19949) Right

In late February 1942, the *Maryland*, together with the *Tennesee* (BB-43) and *Colorado* (BB-45), departed Puget Sound for San Francisco. There the three joined the *Mississippi* (BB-41) which had steamed from the Atlantic, in a period of intensive training with Adm. Pye's Task Force 1, now made up of the Pacific Fleet's four available battleships and a destroyer screen. For five months, the *Maryland* was in and out of West Coast ports and undertook numerous cruises, including one toward the Christmas Islands. When reports of the Battle of Midway came in on June 5, Pye sortied from San Francisco with the *Maryland, Colorado*, the escort carrier *Long Island* (AVG-1), and destroyers. This force steamed to an area about 1,200 miles northeast of Hawaii and the same distance west of San Francisco anticipating that part of Adm. Yamamoto's fleet might try an "end run" raid on the West Coast. On June 14, after the defeated Japanese were clearly back in their home waters, Pye ordered his force back to Pearl Harbor.

On Aug. 1, 1942, Task Force 1 set off for a week of exercises. Pye's battleships then joined the *Hornet* (CV-8)—on her way to support the Guadalcanal operation—and escorted the carrier as far as Hawaii, where the old battleships entered the harbor en masse. With officers and men in their whites at division parade, the *Maryland* and her sisters made an impressive entrance on their first return to the site of the Dec. 7 disaster. At Pearl, the *Maryland* received aboard the new commander of BatDiv 4, Rear Adm. Harry W. Hill, the same officer who four years earlier had written of her silver service.

In company with the *Colorado*, the *Maryland* departed southward in early November, for the forward area. BatDiv 4 operated at first out of the Fiji Islands in support of the Guadalcanal campaign, and was assigned to sentinel duty along the lower supply routes to Australia. Several times hints were received of possible Japanese moves into the area and each time Hill's dreadnoughts steamed from the British possession to search the seas, finding nothing.

On Jan. 14, 1943, Capt. Godwin was relieved by Capt. C.H. Jones. Back in November, as the *Maryland* had crossed the Equator and her men had faced King Neptune's justice, Godwin had addressed the crew and warned that some of the ship's company would not return. All aboard were saddened to learn that Godwin himself was the first to fulfill that prophecy; in February, as BatDiv 4 was enroute to the New Hebrides for additional guard duty, word came in that the *Maryland's* former skipper had died in the crash, near San Francisco, of his homeward-bound transport plane.

The mostly-idle 6½ month tour Hill's ships spent in the "Tropical paradise" at the New Hebrides was anything but pleasant. The men had to deal with flies, intolerable heat, and the crude liberty facilities of the growing base at Efat. In August, the *Maryland* and *Colorado* departed for Hawaii and a five week overhaul. In September, Adm. Hill was given command of Amphibious Group 2 and plunged into the planning for the *Maryland's* first offensive action of the war, "Operation Galvanic."

The *Maryland* departed the Hawaiian Islands on October 20, 1943, steaming once more to the New Hebrides. When she arrived in Havannah Harbor, she still had 20 shipyard workmen on board who were making alterations to enable the ship to serve

Officers in conference aboard the Maryland *during the attack on Tarawa. Left to right, front row: Col. M.A. Eden, USMC, Brig. Gen. Thomas L. Bourke, USMC, Rear Adm. Harry W. Hill, USN, Maj. Gen. Julian C. Smith, USMC, (back row) Capt. T.J. Ryan, USN, and Capt. J.R. Tate, USN.*   USN

as command center for the upcoming Tarawa operation. Most of the improvements centered around the installation of a communication center on a wing of the flag bridge. It was the only available place where the tremendous amount of electrical and electronic work could be completed in time for the campaign. But the flag bridge, unfortunately, was at about the same level as the muzzles of the 16-inch forward guns when they were firing at moderate (shore) range. This introduced the hazard that all communications might be interrupted by the guns' blast.

In late October, Adm. Hill's flag (commander, Southern Attack Force [Task Force 53]), was hoisted aboard as was that of Rear Adm. Laurence T. Dubose, boss of Fire Support Section II (TF 53.4.2), which included the *Maryland*. Following pre-invasion practice, the admirals and their staffs were joined aboard by Maj. Gen. Julian C. Smith, commander of the 2nd Marine Division, and his staff. Attached to Smith's staff as an observer was the noted commando, Lt. Col. Evans F. Carlson. Meanwhile, far to the north and almost directly atop the Equator, Rear Adm. Keiji Shibasaki told his 2,600 dug-in defenders: "A million men cannot take Tarawa in a hundred years!"

The *Maryland, Tennessee*, and *Colorado*, along with four cruisers, an escort carrier group, and nine destroyers, departed their staging area on Nov. 12. With them were 16 transports carrying the 18,600 Marines and their equipment. In the early morning

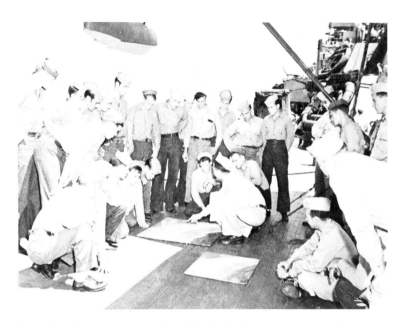

Instructions in turret operations aboard the Maryland *prior to Tarawa attack.*   USN

Gen. Julian C. Smith, USMC, and Rear Adm. H.W. Hill watch the action during the bombardment of Tarawa.   USN

of Nov. 20, the *Maryland* arrived off Betio Island, the main objective of the atoll. Hill's flagship was greeted by fire from two 8-inchers on the southwestern point of the two-mile-long island. Almost immediately, the *Maryland's* main battery responded in kind, silencing the Japanese gunners with 10 16-inch salvos. An hour after her arrival, the *Maryland* opened her scheduled bombardment of the landing area.

The American plan called for Betio to undergo a concentration of naval and aerial attack that at the time was unsurpassed in the history of war. "Gentlemen," the Marines were told by overall fire support chief Rear Adm. Howard F. Kingman, "we will not neutralize Betio. We will not destroy it. We will obliterate it!" After weeks of strikes by the 7th Air Force's B-24s, the island would be subjected to bombing runs from fleet- and escort-carrier aircraft in addition to a naval bombardment so intense that 3,000 tons of shells—some 10 tons of high explosives per acre—were to fall on an island less than half the size of New York's Central Park. All of this would be followed by the leatherneck assault.

Early on D day, Nov. 20, the *Maryland* moved close in to Betio; it was hoped that her exposed position would draw non-damaging Japanese fire and reveal the location of hidden batteries. The orders for the day read: "0620 commence scheduled bombardment. Give the bastards Hell!" For 35 minutes, the *Maryland's* main and secondary cannon joined those from other bombardment ships in hammering away at pillboxes, gun emplacements, control points, and other installations. Then the grand landing design began to unravel.

Ceasing fire for an anticipated air strike, sailors aboard the *Maryland* from Hill downward, were astonished when the planes did not show up; somehow, the carriers and bombardment ships were operating on different schedules. Trying to raise the tardy planes, the admiral found that concussions from the 16-inchers had damaged his radio equipment. While he waited, Japanese gunners took advantage of the lull to fire on the Marine transports, which were unloading troops, forcing the initial assault waves to steam farther offshore. Finally, Hill ordered the fire ships to turn their guns loose on the island; this pressure was maintained until the U.S. planes showed up to deliver their impressive, but ineffective, strike. The naval bombardment then recommenced in support of the incoming invasion waves, which were due to hit the beach at 0830.

Lt. Cmdr. Robert A. MacPherson, flying one of the *Maryland's* spotters, reported that the choppy lagoon waters, with their strong currents, were delaying the approach of the assault craft, a report confirmed by the minesweeper *Pursuit* (AM-108). The admiral was thus forced to advance H-hour, a move which created more timing problems. The bombardment and strafing runs, designed to keep the defenders hiding, were supposed to continue until just before the Marines landed. But, because of further confusion over which element was to be attacking when (much of it due to the *Maryland's* erratic radios) the gunfire and bombing ended 18 minutes early. Despite the great weight of the American pounding, most of the protected Japanese machine gun positions survived, and Adm. Shibasaki's troops, free from U.S. bombs and shells, made ready to destroy the invaders at the water's edge.

Approaching the beach at 0900, the first wave of Marines landed and some units fought their way to the airstrip. The second and third waves met heavy opposition and many leathernecks were killed by a lethal cross fire from the Japanese machine guns. Although a foothold was gained, the operation bogged down in stiff fighting only yards inland. A reef effectively barred landing boats from approaching closer, and troops wading ashore were either slaughtered or arrived in a state of complete disorganization. On top of this, the island initially was covered with so much smoke from bombs, shells, and burning emplacements that it proved difficult, even from the air, to see very much. At one point, assault force boss Col. David Shoup had to ask observer Carlson to make his way back to the *Maryland* to give the brass an idea of what was happening. After several adventures, the noted raider arrived aboard and gave Smith and Hill their first complete picture of the situation ashore.

The *Maryland*'s gunners, after wiping out several machine gun nests, were ordered to stand down in hopes that less shock would assist communications. As men came and went with orders and information, pilot MacPherson and his colleague, Lt. j.g. F.C. Whaley, circled the shore trying to observe the battle's progress. Whaley on several occasions attacked Japanese positions with hand grenades and machine gun fire, actions which forced the enemy to retaliate with bullets that punctured the Kingfisher and wounded the radioman.

At dusk, the battleships and cruisers withdrew for the night to an area southwest of Betio; ashore, bitter fighting raged. On the *Maryland*'s deck, sailors listened and watched, noting occasional flashes from artillery and flame-throwers.

Early on Nov. 21, the heavy ships returned to their fire support area to provide anti-aircraft protection for the transports and to await call-fire requests. The *Maryland*'s

float planes again circled the island and by 1600, after a day and a half of bitter fighting, Col. Shoup signalled: "We are winning!" Betio was finally secured by the afternoon of Nov. 23; 1,009 Marines and all but 17 of the Japanese died in the fight.

The failure of communications aboard the *Maryland* during the Betio landing probably contributed to the loss of American lives. The close proximity of the flag bridge transmitters, receivers, and antennae caused mutual interference, and, as feared earlier, several of her communications installations were so damaged by the shock of her 16-inchers as to be completely inoperative. Furthermore, had the *Maryland* been forced to leave the Tarawa region to engage in a surface action, for instance, the ability of Adm. Hill and Gen. Smith to exercise command might have been seriously impaired. All of these shortcomings confirmed that a battleship—any battleship—was no substitute for an amphibious command ship. None were yet available, however, and the *Maryland*, as the only alternative at hand, performed as well, or better than, expected.

On Dec. 7, the ship departed Tarawa for Pearl Harbor. On the 15th, just after Capt. Jones was relieved by Capt. Herbert J. Ray, she headed for San Francisco with the *Colorado* and *Tennessee*. Although the visit to the city was very short, it enabled many men who lived nearby to get home for the Christmas holidays. On Dec. 29, the *Maryland* began intensive bombardment practice, pounding San Clemente Island in rehearsal for the invasion of the Marshall Islands in the upcoming "Operation Flintlock."

Tarawa beaches during bombardment as seen from the Maryland.   USN

Secondary battery firing. USN

Loading ammo into Higgins boats for transfer to destroyers shelling beach. USN

Main battery in action. USN

5" AA battery in action. USN

Over the holidays, admirals Hill and Dubose moved to new assignments. The new Fire Support Group, consisting of the *Maryland* and several other vessels, was formed under the guidance of Rear Adm. Jesse Oldendorf. Rear Adm. Thomas D. Ruddock was aboard the *Maryland* as boss of the battleship element, Task Unit 53.5.1. Early on Jan. 14, 1944, Ruddock's division departed California for Hawaii, where Rear Adm. Richard L. Connolly, a veteran of the Sicily-Salerno landings, was forming a Northern Attack Force (Task Force 53) for the assault on Roi-Namur. These were the causeway-connected islands at the northern tip of Kwajalein atoll—the world's longest atoll and site of a major Japanese airfield.

During the night of Jan. 30, the *Maryland* drew into position off Roi where, as the result of carrier raids, great fires could be seen in the pre-dawn hours. At sunrise the ship steamed to within 2,000 yards of the beach, and shortly thereafter commenced a general area bombardment which chewed up both exposed and camouflaged Japanese positions.

In late morning, Adm. Connolly signalled: "Desire *Maryland* move in really close this afternoon for counter-battery and counter blockhouse fire . . . " This message earned the admiral his nickname of "Close-in" Connolly and resulted in the battleship's positioning herself within 1,000 yards of shore. Her main and secondary fire now became so intensive that the liners of No. 1 turret split. Hardly a tree was left standing, but over half the island's hidden defenders survived. They would be killed—almost one by one—in fierce combat lasting until Feb. 1.

After the 4th Marine Division had the ground victory, Connolly made the *Maryland* his flagship and praised her gunnery as "accurate and effective, having achieved the successful destruction of the enemy's organized defense." By Feb. 7, all of Kwajalein atoll was in American hands. The lessons learned since Tarawa helped to keep the toll down to 372 U.S. dead. A week later, the *Maryland* departed, via Hawaii, for Bremerton and her second remodeling.

Renewed, the *Maryland* returned to Pearl Harbor for the largest campaign of the Pacific war yet attempted—the capture of Saipan in the Marianas. Mooring at Pearl Harbor's "Fox 5," where she had escaped almost unhurt on Dec. 7, 1941, the ship was soon assigned to Fire Support Group One (TG 52.17) under Adm. Oldendorf. After a week of intensive shore bombardment rehearsals off Maui and Kahoolawe, Oldendorf's ships departed Hawaiian waters for Kwajalein. In Roi lagoon, site of her earlier "close-in" gunnery exhibition, the battlewagon joined others in preparing for Vice Adm. Richmond K. Turner's "Operation Forager."

On June 10, 1944, the *Maryland* (with Adm. Ruddock embarked) and her task group left their forward anchorage. En route, the sailors listening to Japanese radio broadcasts for amusement heard the suave propaganda voice of Tokyo Rose blandly announce that the defenders of Saipan, led by the same Vice Adm. Nagumo who had bombed Pearl Harbor, were eagerly awaiting the American arrival.

Reveille sounded aboard the *Maryland* an hour before dawn on June 14. Clothed in fresh garments and their chow consumed, many hands were at their stations before

Sailing into the port at Efate in the South Pacific.   Frank Mitchell

Antics during the crossing of the Equator.   Frank Mitchell

the general quarters sounded. Rounding Saipan's northern tip, Capt. Ray's vessel launched her float planes and gingerly maneuvered into position off Mutcho Point and Maniagassa Island. With directors on target and the main batteries trained out, the standby buzzer went off in the turrets. Then, at precisely 0548, a salvo was fired. Two coast defense guns on Maniagassa immediately fell victim to the *Maryland*'s high capacity (HC) bombardment shells while more HC shells leveled all sorts of facilities and emplacements in the village of Garapan, raising clouds of smoke and dust. The invasion of June 15 was successful and the warship, her preliminary shelling finished, stood by for call-fire in support of the troops.

In an effort to turn the Americans away, Japanese admirals attempted a naval relief of the Marianas. Departing the beaches at daylight on June 17, the *Maryland* joined others of Oldendorf's task group in a patrol west of Saipan. Over the next three days, planes from Task Force 58 wiped out the Imperial naval air force in what American carrier men later called the "Marianas Turkey Shoot." On June 22, the U.S. battleships dropped anchor for the night off the southeast coast of the island and here the Japanese obtained some measure of revenge for their recent aerial defeat.

Just after dusk, a lone Mitsubishi G4M "Betty," undetected by radar, flew low over the Saipan hills. The Americans heard the plane as it zoomed into a sharp bank and then sighted it when the plane appeared off the bow of the *Pennsylvania* (BB-38), anchored 600 yards off the *Maryland*'s port side. Suddenly the bomber headed for the parked battleships, and dropped a torpedo into the water a few yards from the *Pennsylvania*'s starboard bow. As the plane flew away, the torpedo slammed into the port side of the *Maryland*'s bow with a loud explosion. Immediately, general quarters and the emergency klaxon were sounded and crewmen rushed to their battle stations.

The torpedo's blast ripped open a large hole in the hull and killed two men. Aviation gasoline vapors rapidly spread into nearby compartments, but miraculously, no explosion resulted. It soon became apparent that a bulkhead forward of the collision bulkhead was firmly separating the rest of the ship from the sea. Damage control parties soon had the situation in hand and shortly thereafter the *Maryland* weighed anchor. Once Adm. Ruddock had transferred his flag and staff to the *Colorado*, the *Maryland*, with Turner's blessing steamed to Eniwetok, accompanied by the *Tennessee* plus two destroyers. Two days into this voyage, Chaplain C.M. Sitler officiated at the funeral for Seaman 1/c R.N. Woolridge and Seaman 1/c F.R. Bone, who were buried at sea. The press in Japan, meanwhile, reported the *Maryland* had sunk.

Temporary repairs were made at Eniwetok, but more permanent work was required. The ship carefully plowed her way back to Pearl Harbor with damage control parties keeping a continuous watch for any weakening of the structure around the damaged area. On July 10, the ship was dry-docked at Pearl, where a new bow was built and welded in place within 34 days. At one point during the repairs, Bob Hope and his USO troupe came on board to entertain the crew, the comedian getting a quick post-show lesson in 40 mm operation from a trainer's seat on one of the mounts.

With a large task group, the *Maryland* departed Hawaii on Aug. 13 for the Solomon Islands. The ships anchored in Purvis Bay, off Florida Island, where they remained for about two weeks. The amusements here for the crews were particularly dismal; however, a visit from Carole Landis' USO group did much to break the monotony. During this period, Adm. Ruddock returned aboard and Adm. Oldendorf renewed his fire support group for a Sept. 6 departure. The target was the Palaus Islands, just north of

Torpedo damage to bow. In drydock at Pearl Harbor.   USN

Officers viewing damage at Pearl Harbor. Left to right: Cmdr. R.B. Goldman, Radm. Arthur C. Davis, Adm. Raymond A. Spruance and Capt. Herbert J. Ray, 19 December 1944.   USN

Capt. H.J. Ray and Damage Control Officer, Lt. Cmdr. O.E. Poole, inspect damage at Pearl Harbor. USN

Replacing old bow section in drydock. USN

the Equator at the western end of the Carolines.

Early on the morning of Sept. 12, Oldendorf's group approached the Palaus, intent upon tackling the small southern islands of Angaur and Peleliu. About 0630, the *Maryland* began an area bombardment of Peleliu's landing beaches, steadily closing to very short range. Carrier planes and naval vessels took turns pounding the tiny island until the assault waves went ashore on the 15th. The greatest difficulty for the *Maryland* in this operation was the location of the extremely well-camouflaged Japanese gun positions. General area fire was continuous enough to blister the paint on the ship's smaller-caliber gun barrels.

As the invading 1st Marine Division quickly learned on D day, the battle for this island would be one of the most bitter of the war. Toward the end of September, the *Maryland* departed for Manus in the Admiralty Islands, leaving it to others to assist the troops ashore. Organized resistance ended on Thanksgiving Day; the entire 5,300-man Peleliu garrison had been annihilated at the cost of 1,950 American lives—almost as many as were lost in the assault on Omaha Beach.

The *Maryland* steamed into Seeadler Harbor on Oct. 1; here units of Vice Adm. Thomas Kinkaid's 7th Fleet were gathering for the upcoming Philippine campaign. The completely rebuilt *West Virginia* (BB-48) arrived a week later for her first post-December 7 action. The two sisters would be among the six older battleships (now a navy class, OBB) assigned to Oldendorf's Fire Support Group (TG 77.2). Rear Adm. Ruddock would direct the *Maryland*, *West Virginia*, and *Mississippi* of TU 77.2.1 under the overall guidance of Rear Adm. George Weyler's TU 77.1. This was part of Rear Adm. Daniel Barbey's Northern Attack Force.

The objective was the bombardment of the Red and White beaches near Tacloban, Leyte, in support and preparation for the landing of the U.S. Army's 24th Infantry Division. The time had come to redeem Gen. MacArthur's famous pledge, "I Shall Return."

The 600 vessels of Kinkaid's armada sortied on Oct. 12, arriving off Leyte Gulf five days later. Following preliminary minesweeping, the *Maryland*, *West Virginia* and *Mississippi* streamed paravanes to cut cables of missed mines, and followed Oldendorf's flagship, the *Pennsylvania*, inside the gulf through a marked channel. Ruddock's battlewagons, supported by the four cruisers and seven destroyers of TG 77.3, took up their positions off Tacloban before sunrise on Oct. 19. At 0645 they began to bombard the designated landing area south of the town. The *Maryland's* "close-in" shoot continued throughout the day with most of her shells falling along the shoreline in and between the village of Palo Palo, Tanawan, and Tolosa.

Oct. 20, 1944, was the day Americans returned to the Philippines. At sunrise, TU 77.2.1 was back inside San Pedro Bay en route to the previous day's station. Enemy planes put in scattered appearances, as they would all day, and Capt. Ray's ship took several under fire, downing none.

When the OS2U's were on station, the *Maryland* joined her two sisters in opening the pre-landing bombardment of the White Beach area. Some 200 16-inch HC shells from the main battery crashed ashore in two hours. At precisely 0900, the gunfire was lifted to allow Maj. Gen. Irving's 24th Division to make its 1000 assault. The landing went smoothly and soon the *Maryland* was shifting her fire inland and to the flanks to assist the troops as they carved out their beachhead.

As the Leyte invasion unfolded, the Japanese decided to strike back, sending four widely-separated forces to destroy the American operation. Vice Adm. Shoji

Nishimura led the 30-year-old, 14-inch battleship sisters *Fuso* and *Yamishiro*, as well as a cruiser and four destroyers, toward Surigao Strait. This was part of an effort to join a larger fleet in a pincers movement against the 7th Fleet's amphibious ships and transports. Adm. Oldendorf, alerted by Navy reconnaissance, responded on Oct. 24 by placing his six battleships, in addition to eight cruisers and 28 destroyers, across the northern end of the strait.

With dusk approaching and a substantial supper consumed by all, Capt. Ray began preparing his ship for the fight that everyone knew would soon occur. Off-duty sailors went below to get some sleep, although several preferred to nap on the cooler upper decks. Others watched as the ship took on oil. Armorers checked the magazine and firehoses were faked out. Unnecessary gear was secured or tossed overboard.

Fire control instruments received a thorough check and radar and radio technicians made certain that secondary stations could be rigged quickly if the need arose. Some sailors lugged water, blankets, and C rations to their stations. Medical personnel saw to the sick bay's readiness and established remote medical stations. After the Kingfishers flew off to a new seaplane base at Palo, a crew lowered the catapult crane. All anxiously awaited the ship's first surface action.

Moving out in line, the battlewagons patrolled the moonless night, moving back and forth across a smooth sea which, nevertheless, surged with a strong current that made steering difficult. General quarters was sounded aboard the *Maryland* at 0130. All battle stations were fully manned and alert, ammunition was readied for instant loading, and the ship made as watertight as possible. Lookouts peering into the dark could make out the other five battleships, all of them survivors of Pearl Harbor, but those below or inside the turrets could see nothing.

Adm. Nishimura, beginning his thrust up the strait, was soon found out. At 2236, on Oct. 25, U.S. PT boats that had been deployed in the passage made radar contact. The PT boats attacked, followed by the destroyers, causing the Japanese ships much damage and confusion. *Maryland* observers could see the distant flashes of gunfire, searchlights, and star shells. Just after 0300, the *Maryland*'s radar picked up the enemy's approach and began tracking the lead ship, *Yamashiro*. The Japanese battleship, plus the cruiser *Mogami* and one destroyer were all that had made it past the lighter American forces. The three were now acting like the cavalry in the "Charge of the Light Brigade." As Nishimura pushed farther into the 12-mile-wide strait, his success probability was zero.

The distance steadily shrank and at 0355, after the *West Virginia* had received the honor of opening first, Capt. Ray was granted permission to commence firing; the range was point-blank, just over 20,000 yards. In the brief battle that followed, the *West Virginia*, *Tennessee* and *California*, due to their newer gunfire radar and in-

A Japanese "Judy" crashing on deck off Leyte Gulf, 29 Nov. 1944. Taken from the deck of the New Mexico. USN

struments, got off most of the telling shots as the six battleships crossed the Japanese "T." Firing full eight-gun salvos while ranging on the *West Virginia*'s splashes, the *Maryland* poured 48 rounds of 16-inch AP shells at the enemy. As the U.S. cruisers quickly joined in, Nishimura's ships began to burn brightly. The flames rose along the length of the *Yamishiro* and illuminated much of her crumbling superstructure, including her 5-inch mounts.

The American battlewagons continued to close the range, increasing the volume and accuracy of their fire. As the *Yamishiro* steamed back down the strait she was saved momentarily when the *Maryland* and her consorts ceased fire at 0409 to avoid hitting U.S. destroyers. Then she was hit by two torpedoes from the *Newcomb* (DD-586). At 0419, the wounded Japanese battleship capsized and sank, taking down Nishimura and most of the vessel's 2,800-man crew. The *Mogami* was sunk by carrier planes a few hours later, leaving only the destroyer *Shigure* to escape the massacre.

During the Battle of Surigao Strait, the *Maryland* had fired six full salvos—just over 6 percent of all the rounds dispatched by the Battle Line. She also had the honor of participating in history's last battleship duel.

The next several days, in comparison, were relatively quiet ones for Ray's command, although the enemy sent numerous land-based air strikes against ships in Leyte Gulf. Late on Oct. 29, the *Maryland* got under way for Ulithi with the *West Virginia*, *Tennessee* and four cruisers. Two weeks later, following a bit of rest and recreation and a stop at Manus for oil and ammunition, the ship was back in the gulf, ready to take up her on-going assignment protecting the beaches and transports.

With the Philippine campaign came a new form of Japanese resistance—the suicide plane, or kamikaze. Four kamikaze units of the 2nd Air Fleet joined regular units in determined assaults on the American fleet, beginning on Oct. 25. The raids intensified into November, forcing U.S. sailors to man their battle stations much of the time. With as many as 18 raids a day, the Japanese flyers damaged many USN ships, although they did not come close to halting MacArthur's invasion.

On the morning of Nov. 27, a powerful kamikaze and torpedo-bomber attack was launched against the transports and warships in Leyte Gulf. The Japanese, avoiding American fighters, struck from several directions at once, while Weyler's TG 77.2 steamed in a circular formation, throwing a formidable wall of anti-aircraft fire. Before the gunners aboard the *Maryland* and other ships could isolate individual targets, black dots dived on several vessels simultaneously, missing most but hitting a few. The planes flew in low from land and then from behind clouds and out of the sun. Only direct hits could destroy them before they crashed or launched their torpedoes. The *Maryland* maneuvered to avoid the torpedo of a plane just downed but the enemy's incredibly ferocious attack damaged the *Colorado* and two cruisers.

Nov. 28 saw only two suicide attacks, both ineffective, but the Nov. 29 attacks will always be remembered by the sailors on board the *Maryland*. Capt. Ray's crewmen, like others around the anchorage, had been under kamikaze attack for a month and the effects of intense heat, nervous tension, and fatigue could be seen and felt. In response to an increasing number of air alerts, sailors manned their battle stations almost constantly; many times the ship was put into a watertight condition in anticipation of a disastrous bomb, plane, or torpedo.

Nevertheless, the day passed without incident until 1630 when the kamikazes returned and the circling ships started to fill the sky with fire. The first plane headed

Damage from 29 Nov. explosion to underside.   Frank Mitchell

All photos courtesy
Frank Mitchell

Bomb hole.

Remains of Kamikaze plane under Turret #1.

Deck heaved after hit.

At sea, March 1944.   USN

straight for the battleship. The plane was solidly hit by the blast of an exploding anti-aircraft shell and fell into the sea nearby, sending up a tower of water 60 feet high. Two more planes also were destroyed and the remaining attackers fled, but, toward 1700, planes were sighted once more and a new attack was on. Just after one kamikaze smashed the *Aulick* (DD-569), the *Maryland*'s luck ran out.

A determined Japanese pilot pointed his aircraft directly at the battleship, plunging into her anti-aircraft fire. Crewmen, certain of being hit, braced themselves in anticipation of the impact. The pilot evidently changed his mind, pulled out of his dive, and climbed away into a cloud.

The same plane returned shortly. While the sailors watched in astonishment, the pilot began to put on an exhibition of stunt flying—complete with chandelles, loops, and other recognized aerobatic maneuvers. This daring kamikaze defied tons of steel flying his way, and won a measure of grudging admiration from the ship's gunners who, try as they may, could not hit him. Whatever his reason, the pilot moments later plunged into the ship's forecastle between turrets 1 and 2, and he died in the resulting explosion.

The kamikaze's bomb punched a 13-foot hole through the forecastle and continued through the main deck, ripping into the 4-inch steel. The terrific force of the detonation carried around both sides of the barbettes, demolishing everything close by and causing damage from frames 26 to 52. Bulkheads were torn open and lockers smashed. The whole area caught fire and plumbing, lighting, and ventilation ducts in the nearby compartments were ruined. Thick, acrid smoke hampered the firefighting and damage-control parties. Although many men participated in the successful relief effort, most of the crew remained at battle stations, their burning ship now a more tempting target for the attacking Japanese. The fire, however, was promptly extinguished and the damage contained before the raid had ended.

Even more critical than the physical damage were the casualties. Only a few of the men near the explosion survived, and they were seriously burned. Thirty-one enlisted men were killed while an officer and 29 enlisted men were badly injured. In spite of the sick bay's demolishment, medical personnel from remote stations administered prompt care to the injured, who were then moved to a new sick bay set up in the junior officers' wardroom. The dead were identified, wrapped in sheets, and placed on stretchers in a screened-off compartment.

A few hours after the hit, the *Maryland*'s crew secured from general quarters and many came to gaze with horror at the disaster scene. Morale plummeted as men realized their losses in friends, possessions, and living spaces. Despite her injury, the ship's patrol continued and high-ranking officers as diverse as admirals Raymond Spruance and Sir Bruce Fraser made calls aboard. The ship finally was relieved on Dec. 2 and headed for repairs at Pearl Harbor. There, on Dec. 30, Capt. J.D. Wilson read himself aboard. He was her last wartime skipper.

Upon completion of the repairs that had begun on Dec. 19, the *Maryland*, on Feb. 20, 1945, began a week of intensive training off the island of Kahoolawe. Here the hundreds of sailors recently taken aboard were drilled in gunnery and those other responsibilities that might soon save their lives. The ship departed Hawaii for Ulithi on March 4, her men drilling almost constantly during the 12 days it took to reach the huge anchorage. At Ulithi the ship joined Rear Adm. Morton Deyo's gunfire force (Task Force 54) in preparing for the conflict's last big battle—Okinawa.

Deyo's force, which included 10 OBB, sortied on March 21. During the four-day voyage northward, gun drills were held aboard the dreadnoughts and, in extemely rough weather, destroyers came alongside to fuel. The battlewagons arrived off the main island before dawn on March 25, while at the same time, Kerama Retto, a small cluster of islands near Okinawa, was being taken over as an advance base. Shortly after midnight on March 26, TF 54 approached Okinawa with its crews at general quarters. At daylight, it deployed; TG 54.1, the *Maryland* and *Texas* (BB-35) together with the *Tuscaloosa* (CA-37) and four destroyers, began pounding assigned targets along the southeastern shore. This activity continued for a week, despite air raids.

On "Love Day," April 1, 1945 (Easter Sunday), U.S. forces landed on Okinawa. To facilitate the main landing on the western beaches, the *Maryland* and *Texas* provided fire support during a diversionary raid on the southeast coast. Following that call, the two steamed around the island to help blast targets with the rest of TF 54. The *Maryland* continued her support duty into succeeding days, although the troops ashore initially were finding little opposition. Only the kamikazes, who made numerous raids, offered serious resistance.

On April 3, as Wilson's ship was hammering the east coast, a message was received directing her to the island's west side. A hidden shore battery had been unmasked by the *Minneapolis* (CA-36) and now the *Maryland* was asked to fight it. With precise handling and six four-gun salvos, the 16-inchers destroyed the emplacement. When later asked about the shoot, the battleship's skipper replied:

Damage from Kamikaze hit 7 April 1945.   Frank Mitchell

That was one of the biggest moments of my career, to see our guns perform so well. After the shooting was over, I received a message from the skipper of the *Minneapolis* that really made me swell with pride. The message went something like this, 'Nice going! I see the old guns are as good as ever. My peashooters couldn't even touch those guns.'

On April 7, reports arrived telling of a powerful Japanese naval force, including the giant 18-inch battleship *Yamato*, headed toward Okinawa. As a precaution against this threat, the *Maryland* and other elements of TF 54 steamed north. The effort proved unnecessary as the enemy ships came under intense air attacks. Planes from the U.S. Fast Carrier Task Force sank six of the 10 enemy ships in the force. Just before dusk, however, the units of Deyo's outbound force still unaware of the air victory, were subjected to a heavy kamikaze attack.

At 1849, while the *Maryland* was buttoned up in general quarters, a kamikaze with a 500-pound bomb crashed the top of No. 3 turret on the starboard side. The turret's 20 mm mounts were demolished, and while the bomb did not penetrate the turret's roof or side, it damaged the top and supporting stanchions. All but one of the men in the 20 mm positions were blown from their stations. Great flames lit up the scene, their macabre glare illuminating the debris and the dead and wounded men. The heat of the fires exploded 20 mm shells and the flying fragments burned and wounded other men at stations in the ship's mainmast and on the quarterdeck. Ironically, radio messages were now received gloating over Marc Mitscher's great victory over the *Yamato* force. The next day the more severely injured men were put aboard a patrol boat for transfer to the hospital ship *Comfort* (AH-6). There had been a total of 53 casualties: 10 dead, six missing, 19 severely injured and 18 moderately injured. Although the *Maryland* remained at Okinawa participating in call-fire and air defense, the damaged No. 3 turret, though usable, was held silent. While helping to guard the western transport area on April 12, the ship's gunners downed two planes during afternoon raids.

The *Maryland* left the firing line on April 14 as an escort for retiring transports. While steaming to Pearl Harbor via Guam, the crew learned that the battleship would continue on to Puget Sound for a Bremerton overhaul. The *Maryland* entered the navy yard on May 8, one day after the proclamation of victory in Europe, and each of her sailors headed home for a 30-day leave. In August, the overhauled vessel was departing Bremerton for tests and training off the California coast when Japan surrendered.

The termination of World War II brought a complete change in plans for the venerable dreadnought. Many of the senior men aboard were transferred for discharge as soon as the ship completed shakedown and had put into San Pedro. With only two-thirds of her wartime complement, the *Maryland* proceeded to Pearl Harbor where more men transferred, leaving only a skeleton crew behind. This crew was assigned to take the ship into "Operation Magic Carpet," the return of American service personnel to the United States. In late September, the *Maryland* arrived in San Diego with nearly 3,000 guests. She was met at the dock by an enthusiastic crowd, including entertainer Dinah Shore, who sang for the men.

Averaging some 2,200 men each trip, the ship made three more voyages during the fall, returning over 9,000 soldiers and sailors to California from Hawaii. On Dec. 1, Capt. Wilson was relieved by Capt. D.W. Decker, who remained aboard into March 1946. The old vessel entered the Puget Sound Naval Shipyard on April 15, 1946, and was placed in commission in reserve on an inactive status on July 15. On April 3,

Kamikaze attack 7 April 1945 off Okinawa.   USN

1947, after guns and machinery were rust- and water-proofed, the *Maryland's* ensign was hauled down for the last time as she was placed out of commission.

The *Maryland* remained mothballed in the inactive reserve fleet for another 12 years. By then, time and technology had passed her by. On March 1, 1959, her name, along with those of her two sisters and the *Tennessees*, were struck from the Naval Vessel Register. On July 8 of that year, she was sold for scrapping to the Learner Corp. of Oakland, Calif., for $676,777.77. The veteran battlewagon was towed down to San Pedro in August, and, after a few mementos were saved, she was completely broken up at the Todd Shipyards.

In the four years from 1942-1945, the *Maryland* steamed a total of 152,697 miles and spent a total of 76 days in actual combat. She expended 3,479 main battery projectiles, 13,972 5-inch shells, and 14,593 rounds of 40 mm and 20 mm shells. During those four years, she lost 53 men killed and 68 wounded. The ship was honored with seven battle stars: Pearl Harbor-Midway, Gilbert Islands Operations, Marshall Islands Operation, Marianas Operation, Western Caroline Islands Operation, Leyte Operation, and Okinawa Operation.

Main battery firing salvo at Okinawa beach 3 May 1945.　　　USN

Recovering observation plane during Okinawa bombardment 3 May 1945.　　　USN

Cmdr. Flathery and Capt. Wilson with war correspondents on board the Maryland *in September 1945.*   USN

V-J Day services on board the Maryland, *14 August 1945.* USN

View taken while awaiting scrapping at Alameda, California, 1959. USN (NH 50170)

COMMANDING OFFICERS
U.S.S. MARYLAND (BB-46)

Capt. C.F. Preston, USN	21 July 1921 to 1 March 1922
Capt. D.F. Sellers, USN	1 March 1922 to 10 May 1923
Capt. F.H. Clark, USN	10 May 1923 to 9 June 1925
Capt. T.T. Craven, USN	9 June 1925 to 24 May 1927
Capt. J.V. Klemann, USN	24 May 1927 to 6 September 1928
Capt. V.A. Kimberly, USN	6 September 1928 to 16 May 1930
Capt. J.K. Taussig, USN	16 May 1930 to 3 February 1931
Capt. R. Morris, USN	3 February 1931 to 21 December 1932
Capt. L.B. Porterfield, USN	21 December 1932 to 1 March 1934
Capt. D.C. Bingham, USN	1 March 1934 to 27 July 1935
Capt. G.S. Bryan, USN	27 July 1935 to 20 June 1936
Capt. L.P. Davis, USN	20 June 1936 to 16 December 1937
Capt. W.A. Glassford, USN	16 December 1937 to 31 March 1939
Capt. G.C. Logan, USN	31 March 1939 to 28 September 1940
Capt. E.W. McKee, USN	28 September 1940 to 21 November 1941
Capt. D.C. Godwin, USN	21 November 1941 to 14 January 1943
Capt. C.H. Jones, USN	14 January 1943 to 15 December 1943
Capt. H.J. Ray, USN	15 December 1943 to 30 December 1944
Capt. J.D. Wilson, USN	30 December 1944 to 1 December 1945
Capt. D.W. Decker, USN	1 December 1945 to March 1946

IN MEMORIAM

These shipmates gave their lives in action with the enemy:

Harold Paul, Alcock, RM3c, USNR
Rex William Andrews, GM3c, USNR
Freddie Ray Bone, S2c, USNR
Luis Zamora Cedillo, S1c, USNR
"C" "H" Chambers, S2c, USNR
"J" "A" Conwill, S2c, USNR
Kenneth Cripe, Mus2c, USNR
Howard A. Crow, Ens., USNR
Robert Andrew Dunn, SK3c, USN
Charles Eugene Evans CTC(T), USN
Eugene Webster Gates, S1c, USN
James G. Ginn, Lt. (jg), USN
James Willis Gist, S1c, USNR
Morris Goldstein, S1c, USN
Roy Petty Hargrove, Jr., S1c, USNR
James Dreadman Harrington, S2c, USNR
William Marion Hathcox, S1c, USNR
Lawrence Loman Hill, S1c, USNR
Carl Clifford Hilton, F2c, USNR
Charles John Hofmann, F1c, USNR
Leroy Arnold Johnson, Y2c, USN
Stonewall Jackson Kendrick, Jr., S2c, USN
Robert Eugene Kester, HA2c, USNR
Thomas Edward Kukon, S2c, USNR
Fargust Earl Lamb, S2c, USNR
Harold McClellen Lanning, S2c, USNR
Arnold Leon Land, S2c, USNR

Leslie Gerald Longford, S2c, USNR
Jack Stephen Lucas, S1c, USNR
Jack Edward Mangold, F2c, USNR
Pete Clovis Manly, HA2c, USNR
Robert Travis Markshausen, FC3c, USNR
Jack Edward Medaris, S1c, USNR
Lloyd Thomas Milligan, S1c, USNR
Victor Day Newman, SF2c, USNR
Rudolph Raymond Niss, EM1c, USNR
William Orville Noel, S1c, USN
Irwin George Nopen, GM3c, USN
Henry Joseph O'Rourke, S1c, USNR
Rufus Miller Overstreet, Jr., S2c, USNR
"J" "R" Peacock, S1c, USNR
Laten Francis Riley, BM1c, USN
Gordon Odell Ryman, S2c, USNR
Harold Arie Scott, Cox., USN
Edward Herbert Seagraves, GM2c, USNR
Raymond William Sturgeon, S2c, USN
Melvin Thau, S1c, USN
Glen Carmack Thomas, S2c, USNR
Hollice Lloyd Voyles, Y2c, USN
Clyde Tennyson White, BM2c, USN
Vernon Ray Wiliams, HA1c, USNR
Robert Murray Wooldridge, S1c, USNR
Vernon Zoller, CBM, USN

Battleship Row and the Arizona Memorial at Pearl Harbor, Hawaii.

Bell from U.S.S. Maryland (BB-46) on the lawn of the Maryland State Capitol, Annapolis.

Wheel from U.S.S. Maryland *(BB-46) on loan from the Maryland State Commission on Artistic Properties to the Chesapeake Bay Maritime Museum, St. Michaels, Maryland.* Courtesy of the Chesapeake Bay Maritime Museum

Roast platter, representing Howard County.

Part of the silver service used on the U.S.S. Maryland *(BB-46) now on display in the* Maryland State Capitol.

Courtesy of Robert F. Sumrall, U.S. Naval Academy Museum

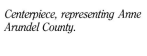

Punch bowl, representing Baltimore City and County.

Centerpiece, representing Anne Arundel County.

Water pitcher, representing St. Mary's County.

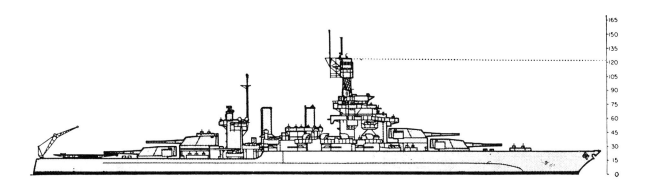

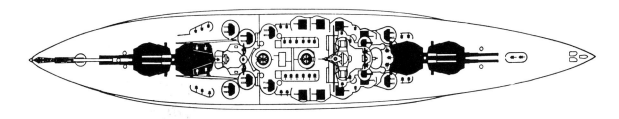

BB—Battleships—COLORADO Class

BB 45—COLORADO

Completed—August 1923
Modernized—1942-43

BB 46—MARYLAND

Completed—July 1921
Modernized—1942-43

Dimensions

Displacement: 31,500 tons (stand)
    39,400 tons (Mean War Service)
Length: 624' (oa)
Beam: 108'
Draft: 33' (max)

Armament

8 16''/45
8 5''/51
8 5''/25 DP
8 40 mm quads
2 40 mm twins
44–46 20 mm

Propulsion

Speed: 20 knots (max)
Max. cruising radius:
    6,800 miles @ 20 knots
    12,100 miles @ 15 knots
Horsepower: 31,400 (shaft)
Drive: 4 screws; turbo-electric
Fuel: 5,392 tons oil (max)

Aircraft

2 SC–1